IRENE

Chronicle of A Survivor

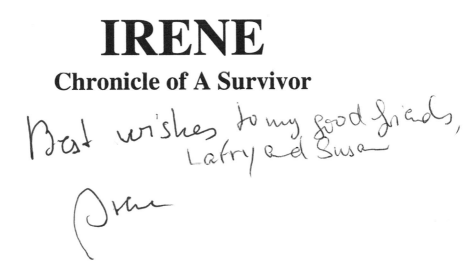

Best wishes to my good friends,
Larry and Susan

Irene

Oct 1, 1011

IRENE

Chronicle of A Survivor

by

Irene S. Hofstein

Shengold Publishers Inc.
New York

To the memory of the people I love who are no longer living,
especially those who perished during the Holocaust.

And to my family whom I love dearly:
my husband Guy,
my daughters Bunny and Myra,
and my granddaughters Jennifer and Deborah.

Acknowledgements

My profound gratitude goes to the following people, without whose help and encouragement this book would not have been finished.

My daughter Myra, who, especially in the early stages, suggested changes, and listened to my endless doubts and questions. My daughter Bunny, who provided me with so much invaluable material not only about herself, but also about my much loved granddaughters. My cousin Stephen, who gave me much helpful advice, based on his experience as a newspaper editor and a writer.

My friend Jean Kramer, whose expertise as an editor helped me enormously. Jason Taylor, who edited and made a manuscript out of all my disorganized papers: letters, essays, autobiography notes.

Adelle Robinson, who not only typed and retyped this material numerous times but also helped me a great deal with her suggestions for changes in the text, chapter headings, and page layouts.

Special thanks to my patient husband Guy, who put up with my frustration, and sometimes bad temper, and helped me make the endless revisions in the manuscript. Through it all he never failed to encourage me.

I. S. H.

CONTENTS

Author's Note

This book is written not only as a tribute to my grandmother but also as a chronicle of our family history and of my experiences from the time I left Berlin as a teenager up until my recent seventy-fifth birthday.

It tells of our struggle to begin anew in the United States, while worrying constantly about our loved ones left behind. It is also the story of our triumph.

Much of this material was written for an autobiography class for seniors which I have attended for many years in Brookline, Massachusetts. Because current events often triggered recollections of past happenings, the reader will find some repetition of thoughts in these writings.

There is a list of People Mentioned in the Text in the back of the book, in case readers forget the identity of some of our friends and family.

I.S.H.

Introduction

I have been reading letters from my grandmother, Jenny Pelz, written to my mother Erna, my Aunt Ruth, her son Stefan (Stephen), and to me. These letters are a very important part of my life. They describe what was happening to Jenny almost on a day-to-day basis from the time my mother and I left Berlin in July 1939 until the time she was deported to Theresienstadt.

It has been fifty-six years since the last time I saw her, gave her a last hug and kiss at the railroad station in Berlin. I have never stopped asking myself how we could have left her there, all alone, in spite of her urging us to leave while we still could.

I cannot adequately express what it means to me to read her words and feel the longing, the love, the anguish. Without these letters, so much of her story would have been lost.

We heard from her until December 1941, when all communication between Germany and the United States ceased—when the United States entered the war. After that time, my grandmother did send a few postcards from Theresienstadt to friends in Germany and to my father and friends in the Netherlands, as well as a list of all the belongings she had left with various people in Berlin, who stored them with the promise of returning everything "when she came back."

In addition, there are letters from friends in Berlin, telling us the painful details of her last days there. Knowing that she might be picked up any day, she had packed a knapsack with a few clothes and keepsakes. But in the end, those were of no use. She had been working in a factory in the hope of escaping deportation but she was arrested and carried off in the middle of a work day.

I cannot stop thinking of my beautiful, gracious grandmother being forced to work in a factory at her age—and all to no avail.

In spite of her precarious situation, her letters always expressed concern for others. One can sense the slow deterioration of her situation and, simultaneously, that of Berlin Jewry. Some of her correspondence had to be couched in ambiguous terms because of censorship. For example, "I must go shopping now because I have to be back by 5:00 P.M." meant that Jews now had a five o'clock curfew.

She told of being forced to give up her apartment and to finally

2

move in with old friends, who took advantage of her and sometimes used her as a cook. We were angry and sad but completely helpless. There was nothing we could do. I have often wondered why we never called her. How easily we pick up a phone today and call anywhere in the world. It was so different in those days. We had no money for astronomically expensive overseas calls.

We tried everything to bring her here. We sold a valuable gold mesh bag that we had smuggled out of Germany, for $500, an enormous amount at that time. It was the price demanded by a man who professed to know a way to get her into Cuba, where she could wait until a United States visa could be obtained. We had heard of people having been saved by going that route, but we were not so fortunate. The man was a crook who preyed on desperate people. The U.S. State Department, known to be anti-Semitic, had no mercy. Each time my grandmother went to the consulate with the amended papers they had requested, something in one of the documents was always "missing." Still, she tried to play the game of ever-changing rules and regulations. It was heartbreaking.

There is a letter for my nineteenth birthday, the first one spent away from her. The warmth and love in every word are overwhelming. She writes on the occasions of my engagement and marriage just a year after I left, expressing her pain at not being able to be with us on such special days.

Among the congratulatory messages for my wedding is a letter from my best friend Marianne, also a victim of the Holocaust, bemoaning the fact that she could not be with us and that we could not even talk on the phone. I still see her beautiful face and hear her exquisite singing voice—all gone up in smoke!

I remember a day in Berlin shortly before I left, when Marianne and I decided to consult a fortuneteller. The woman looked at me and said, "I can't tell you anything," which meant, of course, "I see a horrible future for you." I was young, unbelieving, unimpressed, unconcerned. But what did she tell Marianne? "You will go far away, across the ocean, and have a good life." Did she mix us up or did she see the horror in Marianne's future and decided not to tell her?

I have translated all these letters. The original handwritten ones are at the Leo Baeck Institute in New York City, where they will be stored and made available for scholars studying the Holocaust. I have sent a transcript of the originals to a friend who is co-director of the Wannsee Institute in Berlin that is housed in the building where the Wannsee

Conference was held and where the fate of European Jewry was sealed in eighty minutes by Eichmann and his cohorts. The house is now a museum dedicated to the memory of the German Jews who perished. I cannot think of a better place for them to be stored and perhaps published some day in Germany. That will be my grandmother's legacy, the story of an innocent victim of the horror that befell our people while the world stood by and did nothing. I want my children, my grandchildren, and the generations yet unborn to know what occurred and what we have lost.

This book is also a chronicle of my experiences from the time I left Berlin as a teenager until my seventy-fifth birthday. Inevitably, it also describes the personal relationships among members of my family. Through it all, the memory of my grandmother, who was probably the most important part of my young years and who came to such a tragic end, has never left me.

A Grandmother's Chronicle

This is as good a way as any to begin my autobiography. It is a partially edited version of "A Grandmother's Chronicle" which I wrote for my granddaughter Debbie in 1984 on the occasion of her Bat Mitzvah, at her special request.

I was born Irene Schlesinger in a beautiful house in Zehlendorf, a suburb of Berlin, on March 24, 1921. There were no hospital births in Germany in those days.

In back of the house were two large gardens, one with a well-kept lawn and flowers, the other a kitchen garden, a source of fruits and vegetables. Some chickens and a goat were kept in a corner of that garden. I was raised on goat's milk. I loved tomatoes when I was a little girl (I still do) and used to take one bite out of several tomatoes and then put them back under the vine. No one knew how this happened until one day my father followed me and saw who the culprit was.

We had two servants to take care of the house, a cook and housemaid who also took care of me. There was a gardener for the grounds and a chauffeur to drive us around in the family Mercedes. In the 1920s cars were not as common as they are today.

We also had two big dogs, a German shepherd and an Irish setter. I've been told that one day, when one of the servants was pushing me around the garden in my baby carriage, it started to tip over, and one of the dogs jumped up and stopped it from falling over. Can you figure out why I am afraid of dogs?

When I was three years old, my parents, Erna and Kurt, were divorced and my mother (Oma) and I moved in with my grandparents, Jenny and Adolf Pelz. After the divorce, I saw my father only on Sundays and sometimes during vacations. He taught me to ride a bike, took me to museums, and did many other interesting and fun things with me. I remember with fondness all the times I spent with him.

My grandfather was a lumber broker, as was my father. He bought and sold timber in wagon loads. The wood was shipped into Germany by railroad, mostly from Poland and Russia. This involved his traveling to those countries many times. He had an office on Unter den Linden (Under the Linden Trees), a famous boulevard in Berlin lined with linden trees. Many of them died and had to be cut down after the bombing of Berlin during the war. The street is in the eastern sector of the city behind the wall that divides Berlin into east and west sectors.

My greatest treat was to visit Grandfather's office. I remember a strange elevator called a "pater noster," after the Christian prayer. Why, I will never know. It had cubicles that moved up and down continuously, and one had to step on and off very quickly while it was moving. Although it moved quite slowly, I was very little then and found it a bit scary. I was always afraid I would be caught between the cubicles if I didn't jump on or off fast enough.

Berlin was a wonderful, exciting, fun city, and growing up there was marvelous. Schools, for the most part, were within walking distance. Everyone walked, rain or shine, although when necessary we took public transportation, which was excellent.

We had a super subway system as well as streetcars, buses, and some double-deckers. Unbelievable as it may seem, everything ran exactly on time according to the posted schedules. Automobiles were not as commonplace as they are today, and it would have been considered in very poor taste to "show off" by being driven to school.

The school system was different from the American one. Students could attend elementary schools for either four or eight years, depending on what they planned to do later. If they chose to learn a trade, they stayed for eight years until age fourteen. Then they could either go to business school or earn an apprenticeship to learn a trade. Students who planned to go on to higher education entered high school after four years of elementary school. Tuition was 20 Mark (about $5) per month. The curriculum was prescribed and was the same throughout the country. There were no elective courses except in the fifth grade, when we could choose either French or English as a foreign language. I chose French and in the 7th grade English was added. After completing the 10th grade, we could decide whether we wanted to take a final exam and finish school or continue for another two years, take an exam called *das Abitur*, and then enter a university.

School in Germany was, for the most part, not a joy. The teachers were very strict, usually humorless, and studies were difficult. I was in trouble most of the time because I talked out of turn. Many notes were sent home to be signed by my mother, who was not overjoyed to receive them. We did, however, get an excellent, well-rounded education, from knitting to physics and chemistry. When we were graduated from high school, we had an education equivalent to two years of college. College, as such, did not exist in the German educational system. There were only high schools and universities.

The universities were less regimented than those in America. There were no dorms. Students usually boarded with a family who lived nearby. It was felt that once a student was old enough to enter a university at eighteen, he or she was old enough to be on his or her own. No attendance was taken. It was the student's responsibility to pass the exams. No one cared whether you got your degree in three years or ten years. All that was required was to pass the exams, no matter how long it took. This placed all the responsibility on the student and helped to make young people grow up pretty quickly. Many students switched universities frequently in order to take courses with professors who had excellent reputations as good teachers and interesting lecturers.

Berlin was not the most gorgeous city in the world. It could not compare to Rome or Paris for beauty, but we thought it was one of the most exciting and cosmopolitan. There were numerous parks, lakes, public swimming facilities, and tennis courts which were flooded for ice skating during the winter. In the section where we lived there was the world-famous zoo where the animals were not caged but out in the open with moats surrounding their habitats, like most zoos today. However, this was not usual in the 1930s. Our zoo had many garden restaurants where people used to meet to socialize. On Sunday mornings there were concerts, and people met for breakfast and music in the park. We spent much time there. The children went to the playground, and the adults sat in the garden restaurants, playing cards, having coffee, etc.

The city had many indoor and outdoor coffeehouses, large restaurants, and dance halls where people would meet with the help of various gimmicks, such as a telephone on each table. The tables were numbered, and young men called girls to ask them to dance. It was a fun way to meet. Another place had a pneumatic tube system through which notes could be sent from table to table. As a matter of fact, this system was used by the postal service in Berlin to send express mail from one post office to another so that mail could be received within a few hours. Sadly, I was unable to go to those nice places too often because after Hitler came to power, Jews were not allowed in any of the public facilities. I was only twelve years old when the Nazi era began.

Berlin had many theaters, concert halls, and opera companies which were open for performances year round. These performing art centers were subsidized by the city or state so that everyone, including students, could afford tickets. Many students bought "standing room only" tickets whereby young people could get together at concerts. Music was an important subject taught in all schools, and everyone grew up with classical music and opera. Of course, we also loved the current popular music.

There were a great many museums in the city and I remember, not fondly, school trips to most of them. After each visit we had to write a composition, which always spoiled the event for me.

As a matter of fact, school was not my favorite pastime in the early years. I loved sports, and sitting still was not easy for me. I played tennis, usually early in the morning before the sun got too hot. I was a good swimmer, and my friends and I usually went to a lake or pool in or near the city. Public transportation took us everywhere. In winter we went skating, which I never liked too much. I always had cold feet, but I went anyway because there was a little house with a snack bar where we could warm up and flirt with the boys.

All in all, my life was pretty good. I was happy living with my grandparents, whom I adored and who spoiled me, but I did miss not having my father around.

I would like to tell you a little about how a big household like ours was run. In Germany, the main meal was served around 1:30 P.M. after we came home from school. Businessmen usually spent the dinner hour with their families. Many offices closed for about two hours. My grandfather was picked up by car about 1:00 P.M., had dinner with us, took his afternoon nap, and went back to work from 4 to 7:00 P.M. Stores and businesses all closed at 7:00, and a cold supper was served around 8:00.

Once a month a laundress came to do the family laundry in the attic, where laundry facilities were available (no washing machines yet). It was hard work, taking the entire day. Linens were boiled in huge tubs, then scrubbed on a washboard and hung in a large, airy room to dry. Then they were taken to the mangles (ironing machines), where they were pressed nearly straight. The next day, everything had to be ironed. My grandmother devised an ingenious contraption. She had a very wide board cut and padded for ironing, which was placed across two chairs. This made it possible for two people to iron the large sheets and tablecloths from both sides, making it easier for the maids to handle.

Food shopping was done mostly at the open air market. Fresh vegetables and fruit were bought every day. Milk, eggs, and butter were delivered daily, as well as blocks of ice for the ice boxes. Refrigeration was not what it is today.

Once a month a seamstress came for one or two days to do all the mending and alterations and to make simple clothes for me. All our clothes were made to order. Very few articles of clothing could be bought ready-made. People did not go shopping just to pass the time. They simply went out to buy what they needed. When the seasons changed, we went to the dressmaker and picked whatever we liked from the fashion magazines, chose the fabrics, and everything was custom made with one or two fittings.

When I was about ten years old, my father remarried and moved to Cologne, a lovely old city on the Rhine. I spent my summer vacations with him, traveling there by train, an eight-hour ride. I felt very grown up taking such a long trip by myself when I was only eleven years old, but I also remember that it was quite lonesome being on the train alone for so many hours. In Cologne, I swam in the famous Rhine, which was across the street from my father's house. One day he took me to a very exciting auto race, and I've loved automobile races ever since. You can see how many different things he did with me. He also introduced me to many cultural activities, which I still enjoy. I have tried to do the same for you, Debbie, hoping that some day you will remember and do some of those things yourself, even if you find them boring now.

The Nazis came to power in January 1933, duly elected by the people. Shortly thereafter they held a huge torch parade starting at the Brandenburg Gate down Unter den Linden. It was a very impressive spectacle indeed. The German child in me was quite awed by it, and deep down, I wished I could be part of all the joy and celebration that went on. After all, it was my country, too. But now our world began to fall apart. The Jews of Germany were in great danger, even though no one wanted to believe that this could be happening in the cultured country we loved, where we were born, and where most of our families had been living for many generations.

I shall not go into the history of Germany, the background of Hitler's election, and the reasons why it was possible for this disaster to happen. It is all in the history books.

In April 1933, a boycott of all Jewish-owned stores was called. The shop windows were marked with Stars of David and the names of the owners were splattered in huge letters with white paint. Guards were posted in front of the stores to prevent "Aryans" (non-Jews) from entering. It hurt business a great deal, of course, because people were afraid to go past the guards. What hurt most was the feeling of being ostracized in that manner. Little did we know that this was only a very mild beginning. We had no idea what horrible events awaited us. Despite all this, those of us who lived in Berlin were better off than people in smaller towns, where things were much worse. People were beaten and cemeteries desecrated. Berlin, as the capital, had many foreigners working at the embassies and consulates. In the early years, Hitler did not want them to see what was going on, so we were relatively safe for the time being.

Soon laws were passed banning Jews from attending public functions, movies, plays, concerts, etc. Our former non-Jewish friends and neighbors were afraid to associate with us because it would mean punishment—prison or worse. After a while, it was impossible for Jews to attend public schools. Non-Jews could not work for Jewish employers. The secretaries my grandfather had employed for many years were no longer allowed to work for him, and our loyal maid was forced to leave. Because we were not allowed to attend concerts, theater performances, or movies, the Berlin Jewish community formed their own orchestra, and opened their own theater and movie house.

One day my girlfriend and I decided, on a dare, to go to the movies at a theater that bore the sign "*Juden Verboten*" (Jews Forbidden). We were taking a chance because sometimes the Nazis turned on the lights in the middle of a performance and asked if there were any Jews present, counting on people to come forward out of fear. We had decided beforehand that we would not budge. Certainly, no one could tell by looking at us that we were Jewish. Luckily, we were not put to the test, but when I look back today, I realize how foolish we were. I guess, when one is young, one has no fear.

I eventually left public school and enrolled in a Jewish private school where I received a first-class education and where, for the first time, I really enjoyed learning. The school was situated on an estate with beautiful grounds. There were excellent facilities, tennis courts, a swimming pool, running track, and much more. Certainly, no public school offered such luxuries. The classes were small, students received individual attention, and I stayed out of trouble. It was a day school called *Private Waldschule Kaliski* (PRI-WA-KI for short). Our curriculum was geared to emigration, stressing foreign languages, especially Hebrew, because we all hoped to leave as soon as possible, with many planning to go to Palestine (now Israel).

Those were difficult years. We never knew what would happen next, whose parents would be whisked away to prisons or concentration camps, which of our close friends would be leaving Berlin the next day.

It was not easy to grow up under these conditions. This is why the Kaliski School became like a closely knit family. We drew together. It was an amazing oasis where we felt safe even in Nazi Berlin.

I remain in touch with many of my former schoolmates, now dispersed all over the world. The director of the school, who eventually emigrated to New York, founded another school—for children with learning disabilities—housed on a large estate, much like the one in Berlin. We have had several reunions, with people coming from all over America and Europe, even from Israel. We all remember those school days very vividly and fondly.

In 1934 I was sent to school in Amsterdam where my father and cousins were then living. My father had left Germany the day after Hitler came to power because he was smart enough to know that things would get worse for us. Many other German Jews, including my grandfather, also knew that Hitler was a lunatic, but they felt it would all blow over in a few months. After all, we had been in Germany for many generations. It was hard to comprehend that anyone would or could actually harm us.

I had a good time in Amsterdam, went to school, and learned Dutch very quickly. I was happy to be with my cousins and to have my father close by. It was a good feeling not to be afraid, to be able to move about freely.

After a short while, I returned to Germany because my grandfather was dying and wanted to see me. His death was a great loss for all of us, and things changed a great deal after he died. We gave up our large apartment and moved into a smaller one that could be managed more easily. I went back to school, but a year later left for a school in Belgium. It was a relief to leave the oppressive atmosphere of Germany. I learned to speak French fluently in about four weeks and had no problem in school. The language training I had had at Kaliski helped a great deal.

When I returned to Berlin in the fall, I applied at the American Consulate for a visa to the United States. I was given a number to await my turn to be called.

The situation was rapidly worsening, and on November 9, 1938, the infamous *Kristallnacht* (Night of the Broken Glass) took place. Jewish-owned stores were smashed by Nazi hordes. Synagogues and books were burned. I remember watching our synagogue burn while the Germans cheered. It is a sight I shall never forget. Only the portal and two columns of the synagogue were left standing. Today it is the entrance to the Jewish Community Center which was built after the war. Burning of books by Jewish authors had been going on for some time, resulting in the loss of much valuable literature. Many art objects created by Jews were also destroyed because Hitler considered Jewish art "decadent."

Meanwhile, all Jewish men who could be found, including your Grandfather Egon [my husband], were jailed and then sent to concentration camps. At Buchenwald your grandfather heard the names of his brother and brother-in-law at roll call. Grandpa was one of the lucky ones. He was released after five weeks when he was able to prove that he had a visa for the United States. His brother was later killed, and his brother-in-law escaped to France with Aunt Margot, Ralph, and your great-grandmother Johanna. Eventually, they all reached the United States.

Aunt Ruth, Uncle Arnold, and my cousin Stephen were already living in America. They had first left Berlin for Israel, then Palestine, in 1933, but came to the United States a few years later in 1937. It was our good luck that they did. Otherwise, we probably would not have had a place to go and might have died in the Holocaust along with most other members of our family, including my beloved grandmother Jenny, for whom Jennifer is named.

It's a great pity that you were not fortunate enough to know your great-great-grandmother and that she never saw you. She was superspecial. As soon as we could, we tried to get her out of Germany and into Cuba to wait for an American visa. Many people had successfully managed to do this. Unfortunately, we paid some crook a lot of money to get this done, but he never followed through. She was first sent to a ghetto in Theresienstadt and later to Auschwitz, where she was murdered.

In order to enter the United States, an immigrant had to have a relative vouch that he or she would not become a public burden. Aunt Ruth did not have enough money to do this. We had no other relative here, so Aunt Ruth looked through the Boston telephone book, calling everyone with our last name (Schlesinger), asking if they would give us an affidavit stating that they were relatives and willing to vouch for us. Most people refused, but eventually she found a Harvard professor by that name who, although not Jewish, agreed to help. He was the father of the historian Arthur Schlesinger, Jr.

When I was finally called to the American Consulate, Stephen's father Arnold, who was visiting in Berlin at the time, persuaded the

American consul to let Oma leave with me. He also tried very hard to get permission for my grandmother Jenny, but to no avail.

It was a sad parting at the Berlin train station on July 19, 1939. In spite of all the hardships, it was difficult to leave.

Many of my cousins, aunts, uncles, and friends were unable to leave and were eventually sent to the gas chambers, but worst of all was leaving my grandmother. She was loved by everyone who knew her. She had been not only my grandmother, but my beloved friend, with whom I shared so many good times. She always listened to me and helped with all my big and small problems. And now we had to leave her behind. There was simply no other choice, and she urged us to go.

Crossing the border into the Netherlands was scary because one never knew what could happen at the last minute. We had heard so many stories of people being taken off trains, detained, and strip-searched for no reason but harassment. Luckily, we had no problem. We breathed a sigh of relief as the train finally crossed the border into Dutch territory and we were free!

We remained in Amsterdam for a few days with my father and cousins. On July 25, 1939, we left on a large ocean liner, the *Statendam*. My father took us to the ship on his birthday. I never saw him again. Mingled with sadness was our hope for a brighter future in a new land. Things turned out quite well, and we made good and happy lives for ourselves here in America.

We arrived in New York on August 1, 1939, one month before the outbreak of World War II, which was devastating for the entire world. So many people died in that war—young men who fought for their countries, thousands in the bombings of European cities, in Hiroshima, and Nagasaki, and the Six Million.

When our ship docked at the port of Hoboken, New Jersey, on the Hudson River, opposite New York City, Aunt Ruth and cousin Stephen were waiting for us. I had not seen them for six years. They had left Germany when Stephen was a little boy, and he was now a teenager. After we cleared customs on that steamy August evening, we went on to New York. We were overwhelmed by it all. It had been difficult enough to leave everyone and everything we knew and loved, to come to this new country where we didn't know what to expect, and here we were, in this huge, crowded, dirty city. A few days later we came to Boston, which was to be our home, and we were delighted to be here.

The war started in Europe on September 1, and Hitler's army began to march into one country after another. In April 1940, Norway was

"blitzkrieged," and a month later the Lowlands and France followed
suit. By June it was all over in Western Europe, and Italy joined the war
in the famous "stab in the back." Members of my family, who had fled
to Amsterdam, were caught in the German occupation, including my
cousins and their parents who were in hiding near Anne Frank's house.
The parents turned themselves in to the authorities. My two cousins
stayed in hiding until the Netherlands was liberated. My father was sent
to an internment camp, but was saved because his wife Christine was
not Jewish and managed to get him freed. He was killed in an
automobile accident a few years after the war ended.

At first, it was very difficult to become accustomed to America.
Everything was strange and different from what we knew, but we were
grateful to be here, to have escaped certain death in Germany. For the
first time in our lives, we were poor, and we missed family and friends.
Knowing that we had to support ourselves, however, we all found jobs
very quickly. (The depression was coming to an end, America was
beginning to gear up and jobs were beginning to become available.) We
worked and saved, so as time went on we managed very well and never
gave up hope that our loved ones would one day join us here.

It was not easy to learn English, but the language training I had had
in Germany helped a great deal. We attended evening classes at
Brookline High School and fairly soon were able to speak English as
well as most native Americans.

In 1940, one year after my arrival here, I met your Grandfather
Egon, and we were married on August 25, 1940. Three years later, your
mother Sylvia was born, and we were a happy family of three. She was a
great joy, a cute and lovable little girl. After a while, we decided that she
should not be an only child—as I was—and four years later your
Aunt Myra, another adorable little daughter, was born to complete
our family.

As the girls grew older, there were years of nursery school, public
school, religious school, and camp; of holidays, birthdays, and parties;
of laughter and tears; of boyfriends and broken hearts—as in your
growing-up years. We spent many happy hours together, playing games,
taking trips to New York, Montreal, New Hampshire, Washington, and
many other interesting places. Almost every Sunday, your grandpa's day
off, we tried to show Mommy and Aunt Myra new and different sites
around Boston. We went to the zoo, aquarium, museums, parks,
playgrounds, and many other places.

Mommy was very active in Temple and school activities, and our home was always filled with young people. Everyone enjoyed spending time at the Woodses.

It was around that time that one of Mom's high school friends began to call her "Bunny" because she was so fond of raw carrots. The name stuck, as you know, which made her very happy because she never liked her given name, Sylvia.

In 1960 Mommy entered Boston University but lived at home, since we couldn't afford the dormitory fees. After graduation, she met your dad, and they were married shortly thereafter.

Aunt Myra soon went off to the University of Massachusetts at Amherst, and suddenly the house was empty. At first, it was difficult to get used to the unaccustomed peace and quiet, but after a while your grandpa and I enjoyed this new freedom. We went to concerts, theater, dinners, or enjoyed quiet evenings at home, until his death in 1968. Grandpa had been a good athlete in Germany, having been an ardent soccer and tennis player, and he continued playing tennis as long as he could.

Your sister Jennifer was born shortly before Grandpa died, and he had the pleasure of enjoying her for a little while. Again, we had a little girl to hold and love and spoil. You came along four years later, and the joy was great. Now there were again two little girls in our family. How nice that they were not my responsibility—only to love and to spoil. How marvelous that was!

An Only Child

In 1985, at the age of sixty-four, I became a member of a Senior Citizens' Seminar, sponsored by the Brookline, Massachusetts, Adult and Community Education Program. It offered instruction in autobiographical writing and was titled "Telling Your Story."

Prior to that, I don't believe I had ever envied anyone. But after joining the group, I began envying my fellow members who had written about such beautiful memories of large families—mainly brothers and sisters. Their stories made me aware of how much I had missed by being an only child, growing up mostly among adults.

My parents were divorced when I was three years old and we lived with my grandparents for many years thereafter.

The years during which I lived alone with my mother were the worst for me. Being left with our maid was routine. I can still see myself, one New Year's Eve, probably at age six or seven, lying in bed waiting for my mother to come home from a party. Suddenly, I heard a crash, glass breaking, police sirens screaming. A car had smashed into a window across the street. I was petrified, all alone in the big front bedroom. The maid was asleep far away in the back of the apartment, and I was not sure if she had heard the commotion. I cannot recall now if she ever came to comfort me or even if I went to awaken her.

Yes, I was surrounded by indulgent love from my grandparents and some aunts and uncles, to the dismay of my father, who was allowed to see me only on certain weekends and vacations. He never approved of the way I was being spoiled, probably to make up for the lack of a normal childhood. What it accomplished was to turn me into a precocious brat, who acted up to get attention.

My mother soon labeled me an "unmanageable" child and duly sent me off to boarding schools, starting at age six.

I vividly remember the loneliness in a strange environment at that young age. To this day, I can smell the burned rice that was placed before us, giving me a stomachache.

While I was at home, there were Sundays when my grandparents took their afternoon naps and I listened to music, notably Caruso records. I knew the story of this virtuoso's early death from throat cancer. The thrill of that gorgeous voice brightened my lonely afternoons. My grandparents were true music lovers, and there were plenty of records from which to choose.

I was a voracious reader with an extensive collection of books, and I kept a card file of all of them. I also began to collect stamps. I developed all sorts of interests which I could pursue by myself, which turned out to provide a practical preparation for my adult life. Now I am never bored, I don't ever feel lonely. But I will never forget those feelings of abandonment I experienced as a child and young adult.

I've asked myself many times why it was that I spent so much time by myself. There are many possible answers. First, I was probably a tough kid to get along with, and other children stayed away. Second, although I did have cousins my age, they lived in other parts of the city. Therefore, it was probably inconvenient for anyone to take me to visit them, and perhaps the other children may not have wanted to play with me.

I can still see myself standing on our balcony watching wistfully as other children, probably the superintendent's kids, were playing ball outside. "Nice" German children never played in the street. They went to the park or the playground with an adult. Sometimes one of the little boys saw me perched high above him on the second floor and kept throwing the ball to me so that I could play, too.

I later became a true tomboy, swimming, diving, bike riding. My mother was always fearful that some terrible accident would befall me. I gleefully reinforced this fear, often telling her that "I almost got killed" performing some daring feat on my bike, in the water, or during an activity considered to be suitable for boys only.

At age thirteen or fourteen, when it became impossible for me to remain in public school because of laws against Jews, I was enrolled in the Kaliski School, a private Jewish day school, and was with young people all day. I developed an attachment to the young director and founder, Lotte Kaliski, who was severely crippled from polio. She always took time to listen and talk to me. I found out many years later that she was also a child of divorce, which explained why she felt a strong bond with me.

Like many of the girls, I had a crush on our handsome young history teacher, who was later killed in Auschwitz. I had an obvious need to always latch onto someone who would pay attention to me. This pattern persisted for many years. It was probably due to the absence of a father figure, the lack of communication and understanding with my mother, and my lack of a sibling with whom to share experiences.

By 1933, when the Nazis had risen to power, my father and his second wife Christine had fled from Cologne to Amsterdam. In 1934, after a year at Kaliski, I was sent to a boarding school in Hilversum, near Amsterdam, in order to get me out of Berlin's oppressive atmosphere. While in Hilversum, I walked and played on the beach where Anne Frank was photographed with her family so many times. It felt good for a thirteen-year-old to be in the company of other girls. However, as I recall, I was still pretty hard to get along with. And, as always, I found someone to "adore."

My father took one look at the latest object of my affections—a decrepit old lady teacher with a twitch in one eye—and was absolutely incredulous. What could I possibly see in her? His perspective, of course, was male. She was probably kind to me and took the time to listen to my problems, both real and imagined.

I went home to Berlin after one year because my grandfather was dying. I was devastated. He was leaving me as, in my mind, my father had left me years before. I later returned to Kaliski School, but not for long.

After my grandfather's death, my mother sent me away again, this time to Belgium, to a convent school, of all places! Quite a few German-Jewish children were enrolled because the tuition was low. This worked well because very little money could be sent out of Germany to pay tuition. I promptly latched on to a pretty young nun and decided that I would like to convert to Catholicism. The impressive pageantry had gotten to me. My Uncle Arnold in Palestine was furious with my mother and wanted to know why she had not sent me to Palestine permanently, to get me out of Germany. But although she really didn't want me, she couldn't decide to send me so far away, as thousands of other Jewish parents had done, never to see their children again. How unselfish and intelligent it would have been on her part. I could have grown up with my cousin as a little brother, and it may have been good for all of us.

During my year in Belgium I had also decided that my young nun should leave the convent. I tried to persuade her to leave the order and even talked to her parents about it on visitors' day. This did not endear me to the Mother Superior, and my mother was firmly asked to take me home, only reinforcing her verdict that I was indeed an incorrigible brat.

In retrospect, I am grateful for having had the advantages of growing up in the home of doting grandparents, with all the material things one could wish for, in an exciting city, with a good education to send me on my way, but always regretful that I was not fortunate enough to share all of it with one or more siblings.

Jenny Pelz, 1933

A Very Special Lady: My Grandmother

My maternal grandmother was born Jenny Grünberg on June 15, 1874. Her first husband, my grandfather, was Hermann Meyer, who died at age thirty-six in 1904. Jenny later married a lumber merchant, Adolf Pelz, in 1908.

How was Jenny Pelz so special, so very special, not only to me but to everyone who knew her? Why was she loved so much by all of us? She was warm and kind. When we were with her, we felt the tremendous surge of her sensitivity. We knew she was genuinely interested in our feelings, our cares, our problems, our joys, and she wanted to share them all with us.

My earliest memories are of that warmth. There was the wonderful, loving relationship she had with my grandfather. There was laughter and fun and the feeling that all was well, as we basked in that marvelous environment. I do not remember any harsh words being spoken between them. On the first of every month, however, when the bills arrived, my grandfather would say gently, "Dearest, starting next month, we will initiate a new regime." Whereupon she would invariably answer, "All right, then, I'll sell my jewelry." That usually ended the discussion, with an embrace and a kiss. Marvelous!

Life had not always been easy for my grandmother. She was widowed at a very early age and was left to support herself and three children, which she did admirably. She and her first husband, Hermann, owned a jewelry shop, which kept her away from home a great deal until she married my grandfather Adolf, who must have had great courage to marry a woman with three children—or perhaps he fell madly in love!

I grew up in my grandparents' house, where I lived with my mother off and on after my parents were divorced. Being spoiled by grandparents was, of course, wonderful for a precocious only and lonely child. I felt deprived of my father's presence and not much liked or understood by my unhappy mother. When I got out of hand, which I frequently did, my mother's quick slaps or harsh words made no impression, but one look from my grandmother usually did the trick.

How often I recall many of her words of wisdom, the same ones, I'm sure, that many grandchildren have heard from their grandmothers. I find myself repeating them more and more often to my granddaughters. Wise words, handed down from generation to generation.

One of my early recollections was of my grandparents' kindness and generosity. Their house was always open and welcoming to relatives who were less fortunate than we. I remember my resentment when "those people" were around too often for my liking. I guess I was not a very kind child, and I probably resented sharing my grandmother's attention with others. I don't recall her ever passing a beggar in the street without stopping to give him some money. People used to come to the back door asking for food, and the maids were instructed never to send anyone away hungry. All of that made a lasting impression on me, and I have great difficulty turning away from anyone in need.

I always knew my grandmother would listen to what I had to say. I could discuss all my problems with her and get a reasonable answer. She was a thoroughly modern, enlightened woman. There was nothing I could not talk to her about. She loved to refurnish the house, and moved when she became tired of an apartment. We used to joke that when the house became dirty, she would have to move. I inherited that trait, and others, from her. We often went to the movies together and spent many pleasant afternoons people-watching while enjoying coffee and pastries in the cafés along the Kurfürstendamm, Berlin's Fifth Avenue.

She loved music, especially opera, and had a beautiful singing voice. She always regretted not having been an opera singer. That had been her greatest wish, but in the small town where she was born it would have been a scandal for a girl from a good Jewish family to go on stage. Even if she had had the opportunity, her father would not have permitted it.

My grandmother was an avid reader and instilled in me my love for books. She taught me how to knit and sew, and although she did not *have to do* any housework, she could cook and bake and was expert in all phases of household chores. She was therefore able to train the servants, who often were hired with little experience. I learned most of my skills from her. I even like to iron, just as she did. This all came in very handy when help was no longer available to Jews after the Nazis took over, and later when we came to this country.

Although my grandparents were quite well-to-do, money was not discussed and possessions were never flaunted. Life was lived comfortably and on a low key, and I was raised to know that one cannot have everything one asks for and that there were many people less fortunate and many who went hungry. I suppose, because these values were instilled in me at a young age, I have very little patience with people who place an inordinate importance on money and wealth.

I was never driven to school or picked up by car, except once on my birthday when my grandmother decided to surprise me. She had the chauffeur park the car around the corner from the school. She would not drive up to the entrance lest she offend children whose families did not have a car. In those days relatively few Germans owned automobiles.

In case I have painted a picture of a saint, let me assure you that Jenny was far from being one. As a matter of fact, my Aunt Ruth told me only recently that when she was a young girl, she once snooped around and read part of her mother's diary. It seemed that during the many years she was alone, she no doubt had many admirers.

Among my fondest memories is attending synagogue services with my grandparents. A portion of our taxes went for membership in our religious community. There was no separation of church and state in Germany and still isn't. We always had the same reserved seats, which were included in our taxes. My grandmother and I sat in the balcony, first row, first two seats, and we would peer down searching for my grandfather until he looked up and waved to us. The men were splendid in their high hats, which were worn on holidays. I was often bored when the sermon dragged on too long, but no one was concerned with children's boredom. We were expected to sit still until the service was over. We learned that everything did not revolve around our pleasure and entertainment.

Ours was not a religious home, but my grandmother did light the Shabbat candles, and the holidays were celebrated. I remember all the beautiful Passover Seders conducted by my grandfather and the warm feeling when we were all gathered together. Luckily, we did not know what was in store for us.

Adolf Pelz, 1933

My Grandfather: a Kind, Wonderful Man

My grandfather, Adolf Pelz, was also an important, positive influence during my early years. Even more than my grandmother, he was always ready to grant my every wish and, like most men, rarely disciplined me. I remember how, when I was a young child, I decided that I wanted to sit on the upper level of a double-decker bus. He did not hesitate to climb the steep stairs, although I imagine that it must have been an effort for him.

When I was about eleven or twelve years old, going on twenty, he decided that it would be helpful for him to combine the office and home. He had given up his car, and the office was quite a distance from home. We moved into a beautiful large nine-room apartment. Two rooms at one end of the house were allocated for office space, where his two secretaries were installed.

During the week I would often watch them work, and every Sunday morning my grandfather and I disappeared into his office. He would read the mail, delivered even on Sunday, carefully slicing open the envelopes, which were later used for note paper (waste was frowned upon). I would then type his handwritten letters on his business stationery.

I will never forget how delighted and proud we both were that I was able to use my self-taught typing skills to help in his work. He would brag about it to anyone who would listen.

I learned a lot in those days, and a bond was created between us that lasted until he died of lung cancer in 1935.

I Never Really Knew My Father

Sunday afternoon had finally come. Skipping down the street to meet my father at the corner, I anticipated the exciting afternoon I would spend with him. What was it going to be this time? Would we visit a museum, fly a kite high into the air, or would we see a movie?

At my young age, probably seven or eight years old, I never questioned why we had to meet at a street corner, or why he never came to the house. Not until later did I learn that during his marriage to my mother, he had been seeing another woman, and my mother's rage over that had never abated; thus he was not welcome at my grandparents'

My father—Kurt Schlesinger

house, where we had been living since the divorce. When I had children of my own, I finally understood why my kind and gentle grandmother shared that anger and allowed it to spill over into my relationship with my father. Her child had been hurt and that had hurt her as well.

It was many years later, when she was caught in the Nazi web in Berlin, that she finally forgave him, after he repaid her uncharacteristic unkindness with deep compassion, sending her packages of supplies she could no longer obtain as a Jewess living in Berlin. This made me quite proud of my father. He did not carry a grudge, which is a trait I try to emulate.

On this particular Sunday afternoon, there was a surprise waiting for me. My father didn't tell me what was planned until we arrived at the home of a friend whose child was the proud owner of a bicycle. My father patiently taught me the intricacies of balancing on two wheels. Being the tomboy I was, trying to be the boy he supposedly always wanted, it took me no time to learn. Training wheels were unknown then, but off I rode without any help.

I no longer recall all the wonderful adventures we had, but some remain indelibly etched in my mind. He took me to my first movie, "With Admiral Byrd to the South Pole." Will I ever forget those adorable penguins parading around on the ice, clad in their tuxedos? I've been a movie addict ever since. He took me to the world-renowned Pergamon Museum on Museum's Isle that was built around the famous Pergamon altar, brought to Berlin from Greece in pieces and assembled on site. And there was the beautiful "Head of Nefertiti," Queen of Egypt. I have returned to that museum several times, most recently in 1993 with my two daughters. It never ceases to fascinate me. But seeing it with my father that first time was special, and I have never forgotten it.

The Sunday afternoons we spent together were truly memorable in spite of all the unflattering talk I heard about him at home. I didn't see him every week, and I remember the many lonely Sunday afternoons when my grandparents took their nap, my mother was off somewhere, the maids had the day off, and I was left to my own devices.

When I was about nine or ten years old, my father moved to Cologne, the home town of his new wife, and I saw him rarely, mostly during school vacations. I do remember one summer when I visited him at his home on the banks of the Rhine. I had become an unruly, spoiled rotten, difficult eleven-year-old. Influenced by my mother's constant disparaging talk about him and his wife Christine, whom she blamed for the breakup of her marriage (although he hadn't even met her until much later), I misbehaved badly. They, in turn, treated me with kindness. My father had always disapproved of the way I was being raised in my well-to-do grandparents' home. They tried to make up to me, for the sad fact that I was growing up without a father, by spoiling me unabashedly. They meant well, but the values my father would have liked to see instilled in me had unfortunately not been a part of my upbringing. He was bright, educated, and charming, and would have introduced me to many important aspects of life, but I would have had to shape up had I grown up in his house. The saving grace for me was that in my grandparents' house I saw nothing but love and warmth, which sustained me and shielded me from my mother's anger and bitterness, which never really let up until she died on January 17, 1991, at the age of ninety-four.

Getting back to my visit to Cologne during my school vacation: I was put on the train in Berlin. As was customary in those days, the conductor was given a large tip to keep an eye on me. There was no fear that anything would happen to a young girl at the hands of a German railroad employé. I felt very grown-up and very lonely. The trip took eight hours. This was a long trip for a youngster, but I made it and was met at the station in Cologne by my father

My first glimpse of the Rhine was a big disappointment. Was this the river where the poor fisherman lost his life when he heard the Lorelei sing while combing her golden hair? It was so narrow, not at all as I had imagined it. Being a good swimmer, it took me no time to swim across, which made my father enormously proud of me.

His house was in a suburb of Cologne. Milk, bread, and vegetables were delivered daily by small trucks. One day, without telling anyone, I decided to ride along on one of them. In those days it was perfectly safe—no danger of being abducted. When I returned full of vim and vigor, my father was furious. He had been sick with worry. He grabbed me by the collar, pulled me toward the house, picked up a stick from the ground, and would have given me a well-deserved punishment if Christine had not intervened and stopped him. I'm sure the punishment wouldn't have been too severe, but I have never forgotten the incident.

My mother often used to smack me with her hand, which never meant anything to me. But this near punishment left an indelible impression. Today, of course, it would be labeled "child abuse." I knew I deserved it but was somewhat mystified by the anger. Later I realized it had been prompted by the fear that something had happened to me and the relief that I had not fallen into the river.

In retrospect, I can only regret my behavior even though the responsibility probably lay elsewhere. Christine and I corresponded for many years after my father's death. I saw her once in Europe, and she was always kind, gentle, and helpful in any way she could. There was never a bad word spoken about him. However, she had the same complaint my mother had had—too many women—but she chose to remain with him, as have many others in similar situations. She obviously loved him very much.

One more adventure was in the offing that summer. My father awakened me about five o'clock one morning, telling me we were going on a little trip. Friends of his, with a son my age, were waiting outside in their car, and off we went. It was all very mysterious. After a while, we arrived at our destination: the famous *Nürburg* Ring automobile race track, about ninety kilometers south of Cologne. This was my first automobile race, and I loved every minute of it. It was thrilling to watch the cars zoom around the curves, and soon I knew the makes of every automobile. For a long time I remembered that an Alfa Romeo had won. That event was the highlight of the summer for me.

In 1933, after Hitler had come to power, my father and Christine left Germany for the Netherlands. My father had read Hitler's book *Mein Kampf* and had listened to him at rallies in the twenties, when he had first started ranting and raving, and, unlike most German Jews, he had taken the madman very seriously. Because Christine was German and a Christian, and he had always had many Christian friends, he was undoubtedly advised to get out of Germany. They moved to Amsterdam, and the following summer I went to a children's camp at the Dutch seaside, where I was able to see him often.

The year after that I was enrolled in a boarding school in Hilversum, near Amsterdam, where I remained for almost a year, with many opportunities to spend time with my father, which made me very happy. I had to return to Berlin suddenly because my beloved grandfather was dying of lung cancer and wanted to see me one last time. Later, I returned to my former school in Berlin and finally graduated at the end of that semester.

The year I turned sixteen, my father was working temporarily in a secluded place in Romania, where he supervised the felling of an entire forest for a Dutch lumber company, Again, I was to spend a whole summer with him. This proved to be an unexpected adventure. Though I was only sixteen, I went off by myself on a thirty-six-hour trip across three borders to arrive in Romania. Even for a self-reliant young lady from Berlin, it was pretty scary, and I have often asked myself how they could have let me go alone on such a long journey. My mother claimed, much later, that she had been against it, but my father thought it was perfectly OK. I was never able to verify that story.

When I finally arrived in Bucharest, I was met by Christine, and the next day we proceeded to a small town called Closani. The place where I was to spend the summer was far from any town—in the sticks, so to speak. It was a nice house, but had no electricity. I don't remember whether there was running water. I recall my disbelief when I realized that I, a city girl having grown up in Berlin-West, which in today's terms would be called "yuppie town," was supposed to spend five weeks *here*!

My astonishment soon turned to fascination with the whole undertaking. The morning after my arrival, my father took me on horseback to the top of the mountain, overlooking the forest. In spite of my fear of animals, I was actually riding this frisky horse. My father was so proud to be riding with his daughter that I think he almost forgave me for being a girl.

We went up into the hills, surveying the cutting of the trees, and I watched as they were pulled downhill by teams of oxen and finally loaded onto floats for shipment downriver to the lumberyards. I will never forget how impressed I was by the entire process. I do not remember much else about that summer except that I had a wonderful time. I wore the Romanian national costume and rubbed kerosene all over myself, as the natives did, to keep the bugs away. The summer was an unforgettable adventure and another example of my father's seemingly interesting life.

I did not see him for the next two years until my mother and I left Europe, forever, via Holland to come to the United States in 1939. It was to be the last time we would see each other. Unfortunately, those last few days were again spoiled by me. Was it my mother's presence? I cannot, and should not, blame my mother's brainwashing for my behavior. I was eighteen years old and should have known better. I cannot even recall exactly what happened. All I know is that my father and I apparently got into some kind of argument. I slammed the door behind him when he left the apartment where we were staying with our cousins.

That evening I found the following letter under the door:

Dear Irene [not Reni or Renichen, as he used to say]:

After everything that has happened—or rather has not happened—in the last few days, I took it as a symbol that the front door "slipped out of your hand" and slammed behind me when I left you at the Meyers' [my cousins in Amsterdam] today.

You have let the door close between us! It serves no purpose to speculate how much others—tact will always remain a foreign word to some people—are also responsible for this state of affairs, because it will not alter the sad facts.

I'm sure that you would prefer it if I say no more about this situation.

I think that you should spend your last hours in Europe with the people that you really care about and should not be forced to display filial love where, because of the past, perhaps there could be none.

Therefore, I decided not to accompany you to the ship. In case you

Permission to leave Germany authorized by Irene's father, 1938,
required because she was under age

cannot find an opportunity to say good-bye to me in my apartment, I want to wish you a trip that will be happy in every respect. My wish for your new life in America is that all your hopes and expectations will be fulfilled.

Please remember me to your mother and remind her of my well-meant words in one of my most recent letters which she, unfortunately, chose not to take seriously.

The disappointment of these last few days will stay with me for a very long time.

Your father

I realized much later how deeply I had hurt him. I have read that letter again and again over the years. It still makes me sad and ashamed of myself. It haunted me during the years of the occupation of Europe when I had no idea what was happening to him. He fortunately survived a short incarceration in Westerbork, a camp where Dutch Jews were collected for deportation to Poland. Thanks to his Christian wife, he was released quickly and was able to stay in Amsterdam throughout the war.

I do believe that in the end he did accompany us to the ship, but there was an estrangement between us for a long time. I kept sending postcards but never got an answer until July 1940, when he wrote to me congratulating me on my engagement in June. He told me that he could not write before because of the difficulties of sending anything except business mail from the Netherlands after the German occupation began.

That first letter still alluded to the events before I left Amsterdam and his disappointment that in all this time I had not taken the opportunity to "come to my senses."

After that we corresponded regularly, and he appeared to soften. Some letters were addressed to both myself and Egon. They were always fascinating and full of information, a joy to read. He told us about his life, his philosophy, and asked us about ours. I realized why my mother was always so hostile toward me. I was a lot like him. I remember how, when she was angry with me, she would say, "You are just like your father!"

His letters were full of affection, and I think he enjoyed mine as much as I did his. The first time he again called me "My dear Renichen" and not "Irene" was not until November 1941. Only after I had a child of my own did I begin to understand how deeply I had hurt him. I tried to make it up to him as much as possible by sending him things he and Christine needed and could not get in the Netherlands after the war. I begged him to come to America because life in postwar Europe was so hard. But the thought of starting anew at his age, with the language problem, was apparently too frightening.

His last letter, dated February 5, 1946, was again full of love, but he appeared quite depressed about many things that seemed to go wrong in his life. I was happy that he had forgiven my behavior of seven years before. Thinking about those days, I still feel ashamed. And I regret all those lost years when I could have been enriched by his knowledge and understanding. He never said a bad word about my mother, only expressed regret that she had poisoned my mind against him. I have never been able to forgive her for depriving me of a father who had so much to offer and who obviously cared for me very deeply. She had deprived me of him not only physically, but also mentally and emotionally.

I never saw him again. On February 16, 1946, I received a telegram from Christine that he had been killed in a freak traffic accident. Due to the lack of public transportation after the war, he had hitched a ride on a truck, and the tailgate had given way, throwing him onto the pavement. He was killed instantly.

I was glad that he had not suffered, and that we had made peace with each other in the end. How much I had missed! My feeling of loss was overwhelming because I had never really known my father.

Taking Possessions Out of Germany

In October of 1938, the "Aryanization" of the property of German Jews had begun. This meant that, in leaving the country, we were allowed to take no money, only furniture, clothing, crystal, and other possessions. There was a catch, however.

An inspector came to our house and carefully appraised everything as we packed. He made lists of all items, added up the total value, and presented us with a bill for the *Reichsfluchtsteuer* (a tax for "fleeing the Reich"). That's what we owed the government for escaping from it. The tax was the equivalent of the value of everything we were taking. There were certain items one was not allowed to pack, such as cameras. The eagle-eyed inspector made sure nothing "illegal" was concealed. Some people tried to get around this law by hiding possessions in the hollow pedestals of tables, hoping eventually to turn these items into cash in the United States. If caught, they could have been arrested and shipped to a camp. In my opinion, this was a risk definitely not worth taking.

My mother decided to glue a 1,000 Reichsmark bill, worth only about $250, into a pouch with a double bottom, belonging to my late grandfather, that had been used to hold the stiff collars men wore in those days. If this money had been discovered, it would have meant imprisonment, or worse, for all of us. But money had always been very important to her and apparently in her view it was worth the risk.

Thoughts on Leaving Berlin

We had waited a long time for this day, the day we would finally get out of the oppressive atmosphere we had lived in for more than six years, although things had not been as bad for us as for many others: I was forced to leave public school. We had not been allowed to attend movies, concerts, theaters, and other public events. But we had never been abused, maltreated, or harassed beyond the general discomfort of the Nuremberg laws, which deprived us of some of the ordinary amenities of daily life. Since there were no males in our household, we never experienced the fears of families whose brothers or fathers were liable to being whisked off to concentration camps. Women were not bothered too much up to the time we left.

When all the preparations had been completed and we were ready to go, panic began to set in. I felt a terrible dread about leaving my grandmother all alone, and about leaving Berlin. These were my two great loves in those days. The young man I had been dating had emigrated a few months earlier, and I looked forward to seeing him either in the Netherlands or in the United States.

On this, my last day in Berlin, a beautiful summer day in July 1939, I walked down the Kurfürstendamm, to the Kaiser Wilhelm Memorial Church (which would be heavily bombed during the war). I watched young girls strolling with their skirts blowing in the breeze, and my eyes brimmed with tears as I realized that this was really good-bye. No matter how much we had suffered at the hands of our compatriots, the pain of parting and leaving everyone and everything I loved was almost

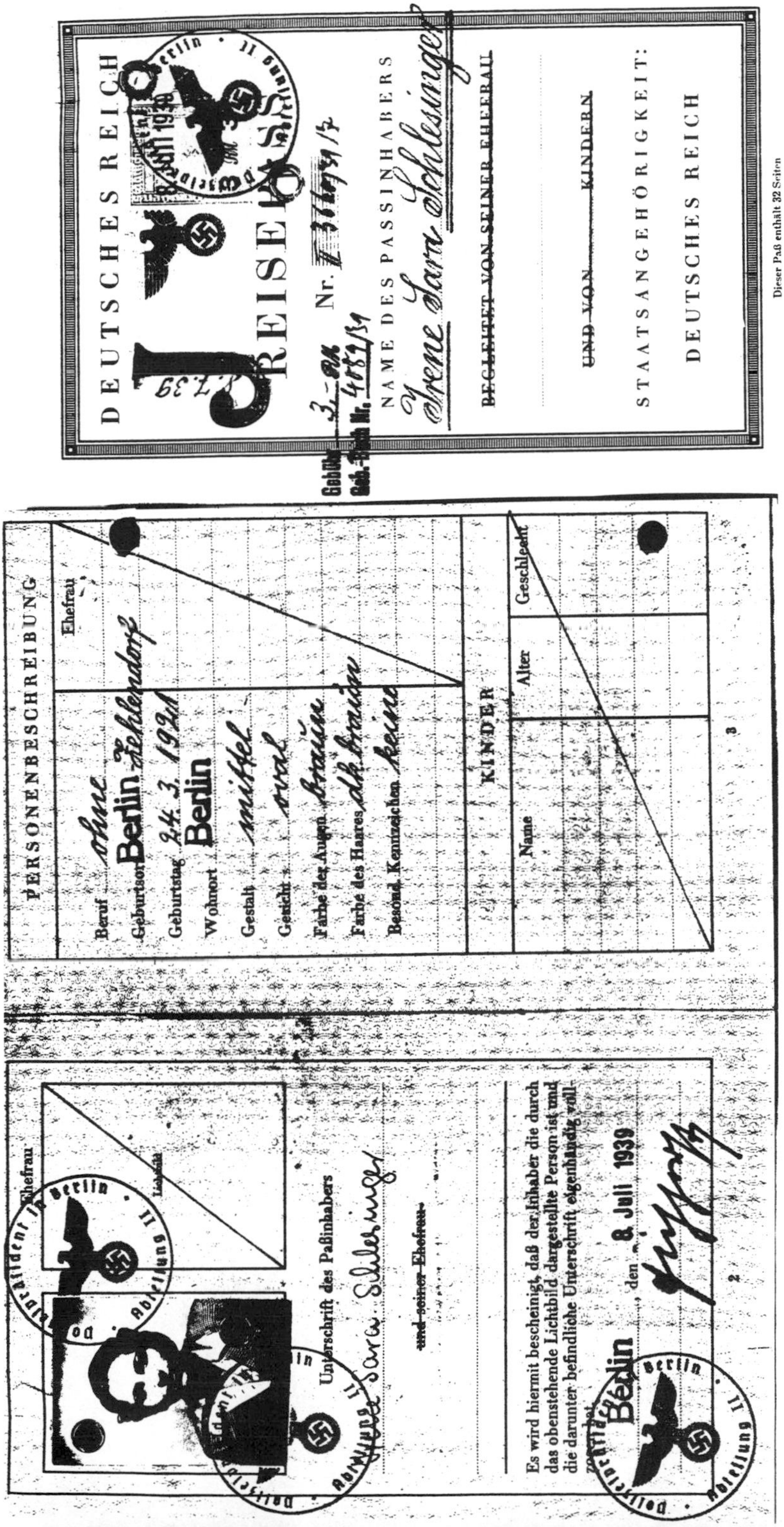

Passport issued by German Government

unbearable. I felt so alone. I had no one with whom I could speak of these feelings. I could not cry to my friends, who were unable to leave and who would have been happy to change places with me. Most of them would be caught in the net when the war started one month later. And I certainly could not burden my poor grandmother who had to stay behind.

When my mother and I were ready to leave on the following day, and we had to say good-bye at the railroad station, I thought my heart would break. I will never forget my grandmother's face when she embraced us for the last time. For a moment I was tempted to stay. I wonder if it occurred to any of us that this was the last time we would see one another.

Finally the train pulled out of the station where I had arrived so happily many, many times, always glad to come home to Berlin. We were en route to Amsterdam, but first we had to cross the German-Dutch border. We had heard horror stories of people being pulled off the trains, detained for hours out of pure sadism, causing them to miss connections and experience great anxiety and fear.

When we were nearing the border, I began talking to a young Nazi officer who had come aboard. I told him my father would be waiting for us in Amsterdam and that I was hoping not to have any problems that would cause us to miss our train. I flirted with him a bit, never showing fear. When we arrived at the border inspection station, everyone was

Visa to enter Holland

ordered to get off with all their luggage. He took our passports, went into the big hall where the customs inspectors were waiting, and took one of them aside, pointing to us and our luggage. In no time at all, our suitcases were inspected quite superficially, and we were back on the train. I guess, even with Nazis, it helped to be young and pretty.

When the train finally crossed into the Netherlands, everyone heaved a sigh of relief. We had made it; we were free. My father met us in Amsterdam along with my cousins, who had left Germany in 1933. We couldn't tear ourselves away and almost paid with our lives. We stayed in the Netherlands a few days and sailed from Hoek van Holland on July 25, 1939, on my father's birthday.

Our ship, the *Statendam*, left at midnight. I will always remember my sadness as the lights of the shore got smaller and smaller, with Europe disappearing from view and literally sinking into darkness. Part of my heart stayed behind and will forever be there.

World War II would begin in only six weeks, plunging the whole world into six years of darkness and despair.

Reflections of an Immigrant

"Well, how do you like our country?" With these words we were greeted as we stepped off the ship at Hoboken, New Jersey, on a hot August day in 1939. The childlike pride of the people in their country amazed and delighted us. We were to experience more of their naiveté when we got to know Americans a little better although, I must confess, they were a puzzle to us in many ways for years to come. I imagine this holds true for most immigrants to foreign lands.

Our first sight of New York was shocking and disappointing. It was dirty and noisy. The August heat and humidity were unbearable. Dirty, smelly subways and buses did not compare to the clean, quiet, efficient transportation in Berlin. And there were numerous other surprises.

Our arrival in Boston a few days later was much more pleasant. Here we found a livable city that was not noisy and dirty like New York. Of course, when we realized that they "rolled up the sidewalks" at 7:00 P.M., we were again disappointed. Having lived in a big, lively, cosmopolitan city, we were used to hustle and bustle until all hours of the night. Where were the coffeehouses and restaurants with outdoor gardens? Where were the theaters? Everything seemed to be closed early in the evening. We didn't realize then that theaters didn't open until the fall. (This was before the days of air conditioning.) We had much to learn.

We learned that "How are you?" did not mean that anyone was actually interested in our well-being. Neither did the question require a reply. And we learned quickly that "nice to meet you" and "call me" or "drop in sometime" in Americanese meant: "Please don't bother us, don't even think of it." At first, we took people literally and did indeed call or "drop in," although this had never been our custom in Berlin. But when our call or, heaven forbid, a visit was greeted with disbelief or a wide-eyed blank look, we got the message and began to understand what people really meant. We learned not to take what they said literally.

At first, my Aunt Ruth and Uncle Arnold helped us as much as they could. We moved into a boarding house on Beacon Street in Brookline, and I cried for many weeks because I found it so difficult to get used to that kind of life.

My mother did babysitting, housework, and even cooking. The last was a real accomplishment, considering her previous ignorance of that chore. In Berlin, she had once taken a teaspoon of water to my grandmother and asked, "Mom, is this water boiling?" She didn't even know how to boil water! But once she had to do it, she soon learned.

While I was looking for a job, I did some volunteer work at Beth Israel Hospital, but didn't enjoy it very much. Luckily, I soon found a job in a greeting card wholesale firm with the enormous salary of $12 per week, where I worked until shortly before the birth of my first daughter, Sylvia Barbara, on March 14, 1943.

I will never forget the question I was asked soon after our arrival: "Did you sleep in beds in Germany?" After my initial shock at such ignorance, I replied out of frustration, "No, we slept on the floor and covered ourselves with newspapers."

This total lack of knowledge of other countries in the 1930s and 1940s, until the soldiers came home after the war, was unbelievable. As it turned out, however, we were just as ignorant about the United States. This country had been described to us for as long as I could remember as "the land of unlimited possibilities." We couldn't believe what we saw. We had thought that the United States was far ahead of Europe in technology, transportation, appliances, construction, etc. Nothing was further from the truth. We were unable to find any kind of modern furniture until many years later, when it was imported from abroad. We were looking for the clean, classic lines to which we were accustomed. No luck. When we wore our high rain boots which were in style in Europe, people looked at us as if we were from outer space. Needless to say, they became fashionable here many years later.

Windows ran on rope cords which not only broke frequently but made washing them an exercise in contortion. That is, windows were sashed instead of casemented. Our windows were hung on hinges, like doors, which let them swing out easily. And there was so much more.

We were, however, pleasantly surprised by the kindness and openness we encountered. People were helpful and neighborly. They were patient with our "fractured" English. Houses and cars were left unlocked. There were no fences around property. Things have certainly changed since then, when this was truly a "kind and gentle" nation.

I feel that our experience is a perfect example of the misconceptions we have about other countries. Even now, with all the information provided by the media and through extensive travel, we still do not understand the customs and needs of people in other parts of the world. Nor are we trying hard enough to learn. Will it always be thus?

I believe that our ignorance will continue to create strife until we take the trouble to try to understand that different people have different needs. In order to achieve some semblance of peace and harmony in this ever-shrinking world, we must learn to respect others, even if their values and customs differ from ours.

The Immigrants' Mutual Aid Society

How well I remember that first meeting in the fall of 1939 at the Jewish Convalescent Home on Kent Street in Brookline, where my Aunt Ruth and my Uncle Arnold Esrati were employed. It was due to their efforts that a place was made available for the early meetings of the Immigrants Mutual Aid Society (IMAS). The convalescent home has since been torn down to make way for a row of townhouses. Many of us immigrants congregated at the Home; a few were patients.

It was there I met my husband-to-be, Egon Klappholz, when he was recuperating after an appendectomy. I was advised not to make him laugh because the incision was still painful, but that was not easy for a fun-loving eighteen-year-old girl.

We had a good time in those days. None of us had much money. Most of us had jobs paying about $10 to $12 per week, but we were proud to be earning that much. We were all in the same boat—young and just starting out in our new country. We were homesick, yet happy to have escaped with our lives. We did think a great deal of our families and friends who were left behind.

The camaraderie at IMAS was very helpful. There was a warm feeling of togetherness, of belonging. We had parties and meetings. At one time we put on a play in which I played a *Freche Berliner Pflanze* (a fresh Berlin brat), a very appropriate role for me at that time. It was great fun. IMAS gave us a feeling of support. We were with people who shared a common background and common concerns. We were greenhorns—together—and we tried to be understanding of one another.

Inevitably, the younger people would later drift away. We married, had "American" children, and tried to assimilate completely. But the older generation stayed with IMAS through all the years, creating strong bonds among them.

In retrospect, I feel that IMAS helped us overcome our difficult adjustment to this strange new land. We were grateful to the founders of the organization which meant so much to us.

World War II Begins

Where was I on September 3, 1939, the day England declared war on Nazi Germany? I had arrived in Boston only one month earlier, having left Berlin just in the nick of time, but the homesickness had not yet diminished.

On that fateful day, I was working in downtown Boston, and the newsboys' shouts of "Extra, Extra" evoked very mixed feelings. There was satisfaction and elation that Hitler would finally be stopped and wishful thinking that maybe it would be over quickly, and we could return home. We feared for everyone who had been left behind. What would happen to them when the bombs began to fall? There was also a tinge of sadness at the thought that "my" country, my beloved hometown of Berlin, might be destroyed. This was probably an irrational, incomprehensible emotion. But there it was.

Surely we wished that misery would befall the Germans. Yet, somehow, I had always separated Berlin from the rest of Germany and, I believe, no one but a Berliner would understand these feelings. Our ardent wish for revenge never included the capital of the Third Reich. Berlin had always been liberal and socialistic. Most of those liberals and socialists had, of course, gone underground or had been sent to concentration camps. And all through the misery, the Berliners had never lost their famous sense of humor. Certainly, all the Jews who had escaped were eager to fight the Germans. Yet in spite of everything, we could not help but think of all the wonderful years of our youth. I was the third generation of my family born in Berlin and the fourth or fifth born in Germany. We had loved the city and had many good memories. But we had not yet imagined the horror that was to come.

All these thoughts raced around in my head as the newsboys continued to shout, "Extra, Extra, read all about it. England declares war on Germany." I remember how I cried—in fear of the killing that was inevitable, in the realization that nothing would ever be the same. I cried for my lost country, for all the loved ones left behind, and, I suppose, for all the young men who would fight and die because a madman had been allowed—no, encouraged and assisted—to conquer, massacre, and destroy.

Many decades have passed since that September day, and horrors which no one could envision were unleashed upon mankind. The world has never been the same. Few of us have come through unscathed.

I have viewed documentary films of prewar and postwar Berlin. They show a great city under the reign of the Kaiser and during the 1920s and 1930s, after World War I. I relived the rise of Hitler, the torch parades, the boycott of Jewish stores on April 1, 1933, the burning of books and synagogues on Kristallnacht. In my mind I once again walked through the streets I had walked as a child and as a young girl; and after all those years, it still hurt. And I visualized the bombardment and destruction that rained out of the skies from Allied bombers and Russian guns. When the war was finally over, most of the city lay in ruins.

Berlin was gone and—with her—my youth. As I watched the complete devastation of a once-great city, my mind wandered back to the day in July 1939 when I left so sadly, and to the day in September 1939 when war was declared. I remembered how I had felt then. Now my overwhelming emotion was, "It serves them right." They started a war—the Second World War of this century—causing the destruction of so many beautiful places all across Europe. They had inflicted unimaginable horrors on innocent millions. The crimes they perpetrated in the name of the German people were without precedent in history. They bore the responsibility and had to take the consequences, although nothing they experienced can ever pay for the crimes that were committed against mankind during Hitler's reign of terror.

My First Husband—Marriage—Starting a Family

Egon's German family name was Klappholz, difficult for Americans to pronounce. The co-workers at his first job translated it into "Woods" (a translation of "Holz"), and we subsequently decided to change it on our citizenship papers five years later. We realized later that we should simply have shortened it to "Holz," which coincidentally was the maiden name of my paternal grandmother.

We were married in August 1940, one year after my arrival in Boston, by the very orthodox Rabbi Joseph Shubow. When he asked for my Jewish name, always the rebel, I replied, "I don't have one." To avoid any problems, my wiser husband-to-be chose a Hebrew name for me. I no longer remember what it was. For me, my new name was Mrs. Irene Klappholz.

Soon Egon found a job in a men's clothing store in downtown Boston as a porter, cleaning floors, toilets, and doing all the necessary menial chores. It was not exactly his usual work. His family had owned a small department store in Magdeburg, and he had had a very good position in Halberstadt, not very far away. He had been a buyer of fabrics and other dry goods for a number of years, the youngest buyer in Germany at that time. His English, of course, left much to be desired those first few weeks in America. When the phone rang, and he was the only one around, he would pick it up and, before the caller could say anything, he would say, "Wrong number" and hang up. When he went to lunch, he waited until someone asked for something he wanted and, always inventive, simply said "the same." But it didn't take long for him to learn the language very well.

Before leaving Germany, Egon had been one of many Jewish men arrested during Kristallnacht in November 1938. He was taken first to the police station and then to Buchenwald, where he was incarcerated for five weeks. This traumatic experience left a lasting mark. He never talked much about it except for a few things he told me.

Always quick thinking, he volunteered to transport the large cans of milk from one bunk to another. Thus he was able to drink some of the milk and, to explain why the cans were not quite full, would spill some on his clothes.

One day during roll call he heard the names of his brother and brother-in-law and realized that they too were at Buchenwald, having been picked up in Magdeburg. His brother was ultimately murdered, but his brother-in-law was released. He later escaped to France with his wife, Egon's sister, their son, and Egon's mother. They were interned in Camp Gurs in France and eventually came to the United States.

When Egon first arrived in the States, he ate coconuts and drank the liquid for lunch in order to save money to send to his mother. I had great admiration for his selflessness.

I began working for a greeting card wholesaler in Boston, a job I held for three years until the birth of my first daughter, Sylvia Barbara, in March 1943. Her sister, Myra Joyce, was born four years later.

I was making $12 a week, as was Egon. After our marriage, each of us was earning the grand sum of $17 a week. To keep it in perspective, one must remember that milk was 9 cents a quart and our very nice two-bedroom apartment near Boston University was only $37.50 per month. I thought that when I got married, I would get away from my mother, but she had no place to go and so moved in with us.

My new husband wanted very much to join the army to fight the Germans, but he was classified 4F (rejected). We never found out the reason, but I was very glad he did not have to go to war.

I had decided I wanted children as soon as possible. Egon was not eager for the responsibility, but of course I won out. I worked until January 1943. By the time Sylvia was born, Egon's English was perfect, and he was making the enormous salary of $45 per week, managing a men's clothing store in Brighton.

I have often been asked if we felt any anti-Semitism here in America. I experienced it once when a neighbor's little girl told Sylvia that her parents wouldn't let her come to our house to play because we were Jewish. Another instance was when we planned a vacation in New Hampshire and American friends warned us that the resort we had chosen was "restricted," meaning that it did not welcome Jews. We couldn't believe it and decided to go there anyway. We had no problem and felt very comfortable.

The greatest resentment we felt was from American Jews. We had come directly to Brookline from Germany, after a short stay in New York. Many of their families had come from Eastern Europe and were living in the Roxbury and Dorchester areas of Boston, strictly Jewish neighborhoods at that time. Though many were on committees pledged to help refugees, they harbored enormous anger toward us: "Who do these arrogant German Jews think they are to move directly to Boston's best suburb?"

I could understand their feelings because I had been told that the German Jews had not been friendly to Eastern Jews fleeing from pogroms in Poland and Russia, trying to find asylum in Germany. The attitude was: "We'll help you with money if you don't stay here but just continue on to America."

I had also been told that many Polish and Russian Jewish furriers had settled in Leipzig, and no one would associate with them. In view of all we have experienced since then, I have always considered this a very, very sad story.

Following are the letters from my grandmother attesting to the years of horror. Also included are letters from various friends and relatives who survived, written to us after the war and the liberation of Europe.

1939

My dear Renilein,

You probably know that Aunt Ruth wrote to me that you are not getting along well with Mutti. Renilein, I feel very bad about this. You are all your mother has and you know how she suffers when you are angry with each other. I know that much of the blame lies with her, but my child, you are almost nineteen years old, think about all the things your mother's life has lacked. Mutti is bitter, her best years were spent dealing with all kinds of problems, and worst of all, she unfortunately inherited the nature of her father, and that is not her fault. But, my dear child, I ask you to please be good to Mutti, be understanding; you know she only wants the best for you. Try to understand her nature a little bit.

Renilein, believe me, there is no one in this world who is more concerned about you than I am, and if you take my words to heart, they will one day be fruitful. When I am no longer here, you will think of my words and say to yourself that your grandmother was right. Because what you do to your parents, your children will one day do to you. So, my Renilein, I ask you sincerely to understand your mother, you know I put up with much from her because I felt sorry for her. She was cheated by life but I knew her good character.

So, my dear child, I beg you not to let my plea go unheard. You see, I am so lonely and only now do I see what my children meant to me, and among those I count you as well.

I love you very much and I greet you and kiss you warmly.

Your Grandmother

December 1939

My beloved children:

Christmas is in the air already and the stores are *supposed to look fabulous.* Yesterday I had a wonderful surprise. The doorbell rang and there was a man at the door, carrying a large package. I unwrapped it and found many things that I can no longer buy: a very beautiful bracelet, port wine, chocolate, ingredients for soup the way you like it, my dear Renilein, and lots of other goodies, along with the following letter:

My very dear Mrs. Pelz:

For Christmas I am sending you my sincere greetings and wishes in the hope that you will be able to spend the next Christmas with your loved ones. If I can give you only a little bit of joy with my package, then my heart will also experience some Christmas magic. I have tried to express some of the gratitude I owe you for all the love you have shown me in my life. I will never forget that I had a second home in your house with your family. This love and admiration has created an unbreakable bond.

With sincere devotion, Yours

Anton (Antonia)

What do you think of that? You see, there are still loyal people around. Everything was beautifully wrapped, just the way I used to wrap her presents for Christmas.

Yesterday the Aufrechts [old friends] brought me a marvelous bottle of cognac. They are simply wonderful to me.

I have nothing else to tell you today except that I miss you. I send you a hug and a kiss and look forward to hearing from you soon,

Your loving Mother.

January 5, 1940

My beloved good children,

I have been in bed now for eight days with severe bronchitis and a cough, and I can't get rid of it. Now I see what it means to be alone. Idchen [a friend] brings me food, but she is out all day. I do not want any visitors because, due to my hoarseness, I find it exhausting to talk. Hopefully this will be over soon.

Clare [Arnold's mother] is up again, but she is very weak and doesn't go out yet. If she does not write to you, it is because her eyesight is very poor, and her typewriter is not usable anymore.

Arne [Ruth's husband, Arnold], you wrote only that you have received a reply from the American Consulate, but no details. Did you know that an affidavit is only valid for one year? It would be better if the affidavits were handled separately. I am sure that there will be problems. Recently there was such a case, and people were told they had to wait until it was time for the highest number to be called. One hears so much that one cannot even believe in leaving anymore. Provided that it happens very quickly, it may still be possible. I do want so much to be with you once again. Like this, my life is no life at all, but I don't want to make your hearts heavy. Unfortunately, you can't help me.

New problems appear every day; today Willi had to go to the tax office for me again. With the little money I have, I still can't find peace.

Until now I have received only tea in letters. Regular mail takes a very long time.

Today I was alone all day, and constantly had to get out of bed. Idchen did some shopping for me and is having everything sent; it is terrible. When one is well, things are pretty good, but when one gets sick, may God help you.

Your last letter was from December 15. Hopefully I will have news again soon. I have no further news for you today. Take care, my loved ones. I greet and kiss you warmly and am with love your sad mother who misses you very much.

March 22, 1940

My beloved child,

I cannot tell you how sad your letter from January 21 made me. Ernilein, my child, take to heart what I tell you today. . . . Reni is a good girl. She is hard-working, fulfills her duties, and is sensible. I do know her faults and had to suffer sometimes because of them, but today when I see and hear how other children are, I have to tell you, my child, that you can be happy with her. That, Ernilein, is why I ask you wholeheartedly to give in. Don't take life so hard. Don't think of what has been, but think of the future and, Ernchen, think of the fact that *you cannot thank God enough that you are there*! Ruth has for over six years not had what you have had till now.

It has been hard for you since Vati's [Dad's] death, Ernchen. But I did what I could to give you joy, and today I am happy I did it. Did it harm you, my child, that I spoiled you? Then I will gladly accept the blame because I know that the memory of things which one has had helps us deal with many problems. That you have not been here these eight months makes me happy because in these months more things have changed than from the time of Ruth's departure until you left. Do you understand me, my child? . . .

So, Ernchen, make my wish come true. Take Reni's good character into account. You will do yourself a big favor and you will make me very happy. Reni wrote me such a sensible letter and that made me happy in spite of all this. I will answer her soon.

I am glad that Arne and Ruth have their jobs. Ruth really does not have an easy life. Ernchen, take her as an example for yourself. She is admirable. I only ask that I could one day close my eyes near you. No relationship is as close as parents and children.

Your loving mother

March 26, 1940

My beloved Renilein,

I received your lovely letter of the 12th of January. On the one hand it made me happy and on the other hand it made me very sad. Renchen, I admit that you are right in some respects, but in many respects your mother is also right. But let's not harp on details. I only want to tell you that I ask you to please not give your mother the feeling that she is dependent upon you. That would make her even more bitter. Renchen, you write that I always loved your mother more than my other children. That is not true. I love all my children equally. It is possible that because of all her suffering and all the illnesses I went through with her, which led her close to the grave, made her grow closer to my heart. . . .

Marianne [a friend who ultimately perished in Auschwitz] called me on your birthday to tell me that she is thinking of you.

I'm still not feeling well; I'm extremely nervous.

Now, my dear Renilein, write soon again. Give my love to Mutti. And warm regards to Uncle Arnold, Ruth, and Stepp [Steve].

I greet and kiss you warmly, my dear Renilein.

Your loving Grandmother

April 4, 1940

My dear good children,

It is eight o'clock, I have just lit the candles, and my prayer was, as always, my plea to God to give my children a little luck and happiness, that they may all stay healthy and that I might soon be reunited with them. This is my daily prayer and I hope that it will be heard.

Mrs. Heller [a friend who repaired hosiery and taught this skill to others] has just informed me, dear Ernilein, that one of her students, Dr. Kupferberg, is going to New York and will take the darning needles for you. I had told her that you need fine needles for stockings. I hope they are the right ones. The address is B.C. Brauer, 108 East 81st Street, New York City. Please write to the lady. [Repairing hosiery was a very important skill in those days. People tried to save their stockings because they were very expensive!]

I received a very nice letter from Jenny [Frohmann in Amsterdam] today and two packages because she is afraid that soon all communication will cease totally. You will probably have to send her a little money again. I truly regret any sacrifices you have to make because of me but there is just no other way.

Jenny wrote that Betty [my grandmother's niece, also living in Amsterdam] is really trying hard to get the Ebensteins and me out. Maybe it will work.

Uncle Willi was very happy with your letters and will answer you soon.

June 17, 1940

My dearly beloved children,

I received your dear letter of May 28 on the 15th of June [her birthday] as well as the telegram for my birthday, which I did not expect at all. Why did you spend so much money on that? But it did make me very happy.

Your love is all that I have left in life, but I will only be able to enjoy it from a distance because I was at the U.S. Consulate in Berlin today and was told that, although I am registered, I cannot expect to leave sooner than three to four years. You can imagine how that upset me. The young man there said that it is my own fault because I did not register earlier. Yes, Ernchen, that was a stupidity I cannot change.

Unfortunately, my money will also not last that long, but I don't think that I will stay here much longer anyway. But please don't worry about that, my loved ones. There is no use banging your head against a wall. Unfortunately, I share the fate of so many.

I thank you so much for your loving wishes. On that day I missed you even more than usual, especially in the morning. During the day I had a lot of visitors [friends]: Erna Babb, Anton, Mrs. Lachman, Mrs. Hirsch, Clare, Paula, Sigmund, Mille, Willy, Anna, and Mrs. Pfifferling. You can see that everyone thought of me. Even Erich and Edith congratulated me; I don't even know how they knew. I received many gifts and had beautiful flowers. Betty [a niece in Amsterdam] also wrote me for my birthday. She complained about her business, which had been very good until now. Everyone sends regards.

I also just talked to Melly [an aunt of Reni's who subsequently went to Shanghai]. They need only two more visas and hope to leave soon, probably in two to three weeks. They wonder why they have not heard from you, Ernchen. . . .

Ruthelein, you wrote me that if there is "still such a thing," you will become an American citizen. How am I supposed to understand that? How long have you been there now? I think that once you are a citizen, you will be able to get me there more quickly. I hope that because of the great successes the war will be over soon, God willing.

Now I will end my letter. I am going to Mrs. Lachman's. Take care, my dear ones. If you write to Arnold, give him my regards. Also write me if you hear from him. I kiss you and hug you warmly.

Your ever loving Mother

June 28 and 29, 1940

My beloved Ernilein,

Your telegram, which initially frightened me very much, made me very happy when it arrived here at ten this morning. You can imagine what kind of feelings came with it. I would never have thought that your child would one day become engaged without my being there. But now everything has turned out so differently and one has to come to terms with that.

Ernilein, I congratulate you wholeheartedly on the engagement of your daughter. May Reni find her happiness at the side of the man she has chosen. And, hopefully, you are also happy with her choice.

Ernilein, let me tell you, you have to learn. You always told me that I was jealous of Kurt Schlesinger. Whether or not this was so does not matter now. But, please, Ernilein, do not fall into the same trap. I have a fervent wish for you, my beloved child. May the man whom Reni has chosen be a true son to you and help you also, and may the happiness of your child bring some joy into your life. Ernilein, these are the wishes of your very loving—and very lonely—mother.

Now, to the second part. Who is Egon? How old is he? Where is he from? Did Reni not act too hastily? Ernilein, can you understand my concerns? I am assuming that all my questions will be answered in your next letter. Ernilein, do the children want to marry soon? If I could only talk to you for an hour.

Yesterday I told Willi that I am moving out, and when the telegram came, I went to him and told him that Reni got engaged. He came and said that his feelings for me have not changed. If I want to move, I should do so, he cannot hold me, but that I should think about it one more time. He knows he will no longer be able to rent the apartment. The people in the house will make sure of that. That is why he was so nice to me. [She apparently had a lot of problems with this old friend while renting a room in his apartment.]

Now, my beloved child, I will stop for today. Give my regards to Ruth and Step. Tomorrow I will write to her directly. Now, once more, many good wishes. I greet and kiss you.

Your loving Mother

June 1940

[Written by my best friend, Marianne Friedland, who died in Auschwitz with her parents.]

Dear Renerle!

Many thanks for your letter. Lore and I were enormously surprised by the news of your engagement, but I'm so happy for you and could cry that I can't be with you. Now, where your life is going to be so unbelievably new, we were torn apart. Hopefully, "he" is now finally the right one. Anyway, I wish with all my heart that you will be as happy as you deserve. I would love to see "E's" [Reni's old flame] face when you tell him of your engagement.

Can Egon support you or will you continue to work? You'll have to be a housewife now, won't you? What does Mutti say to it all? Isn't she jealous? If we could only talk on the phone, but unfortunately that is so expensive!

I'm enclosing my picture so that you won't forget me altogether in the midst of all your happiness.

Will your wedding ceremony be in German? Does Egon have siblings and parents? What is his profession? Please let me know everything!

I'm dead tired and want to close for today. I have to get up at 4:15 tomorrow morning to go to work [probably doing forced labor].

So, Reni dear, I wish for you that you will be the happiest girl in Boston. You can't ask for anything more.

Please give my regards to Mutti too and my good wishes are for her too.

A hug and a kiss,

Marianne

[Written by Marianne's mother, Herta, who died with her in Auschwitz.]

My dear Renerle:

Marianne wished you so much luck already that there is hardly anything left for me. I send you a big kiss for this wonderful event. All of us share your happiness and wish you a happy future. May your choice be such a happy one that you will only have sunny days.

I'm sure it's a great joy for Mutti, too, and one less worry. It's about time that there is a little more sunshine in her life.

Marianne is working very hard, a bit too much already, quite pressured, but the main thing is that she is in good spirits and very cheerful. I hope that she'll stay well and then we'll see. Maybe good times will come for us too.

Take care, stay well, and don't forget us. With warm regards from all of us including Oma [Marianne's grandmother]. Best wishes and congratulations to your fiancé too.

Yours,
Aunt Herta

Dear Ernchen:

Now you are a mother-in-law! Are you aware of that honor? Nobody will believe it, and you the least, huh? But one gets older faster than one wishes. Anyway, I wish you all the best. May the union be a happy one and may it give you only joy. Now you can finally think of yourself, too, and you would be foolish if you didn't look around for a suitable man. Your dear mother would be especially pleased!

My husband and mother send their good wishes as well.

I will close now because the letter must be mailed, but I will write you more in the next few days.

Warmly, in old friendship,

Yours,
Herta

Jenny's last apartment,
Bayrischer Platz 5,
photo taken in 1995

July 9, 1940

My beloved, good Children,

You cannot imagine how longingly I await news from you. I want to know everything about Reni's engagement.

I got a letter from Kurt on Saturday in which he asked me for more details. For the time being, he is not very happy about it. He is afraid, that you, Ernilein, only want to marry your daughter off very young. He hopes that Reni is marrying an American, so that she can bring him over. He would surely be no burden. His wife is going back to Cologne for his sake, just as she once came to him, until things are better with him. He has to be sensible and he cannot involve her in such an uncertain future.

Now, my dear ones, I am moving in with Mille [Aufrecht, an old friend] on August 1. I have been reluctant to move, but there is no other way. I do not want the aggravation here every day. So mail the next letter to Bayrischer Platz 5. I do not think the move is worth it. There are so many expenses involved, but it doesn't matter. I think I will go on a "journey" soon. I always think of you, otherwise I would not go on this trip to recuperate. Maybe I will see you once more in my lifetime. [She is talking about deportation to a concentration camp.]

Kurt writes that he hopes you asked his former friend, Harry Wiener, for advice about this engagement and that nothing rash has happened. Reni should also answer all of his questions. But, Ernilein, I ask you, please don't you write to him!

Yesterday, Hina [our long-time seamstress] came to visit me. I am supposed to give all of you regards. She wishes you, Renilein, lots of luck. Hina will help me move. I don't know yet whom I will use as a mover. I don't feel very good about the move. I only ask that I can leave in peace.

Ernchen, what do you say about Kurt Schlesinger? How he remembers his ex-mother-in-law?

He sees Linchen [a friend] a lot. I assume that is where he eats. Linchen wrote me a terribly sad letter. On the other hand, I have not heard from Betty at all, even though I answered her with a return envelope. Things don't seem to be going well there.

Other than that, I cannot tell you much about me. I am pretty much worn out. My arm is giving me a lot of trouble. And my sleeplessness! Once I wake up I cannot go back to sleep.

Ernilein, I think that you will receive the needles soon and I will try to send you the sewing needles too. Else Pinkman is going to the U.S.A. too; it is her turn now. If the war would only end soon; it is terrible!

It is pretty cold here already. We could use a warm room and I hope we will soon have it. This morning it was 5 degrees.

My regards to Ruth and Steve. I will write to them again on Saturday.

August 6, 1940

My beloved Renilein and dear Egon,

Today I have to send you my most ardent wishes for this special day from so very far away. Do I have to tell you what I wish for you? You know, my dearest child, that there is nothing more important for me than my children and that I am willing to make every sacrifice for you if I could buy you the happiness that I am asking for you from the Almighty. However, it does not go according to our wishes. And so, my Renilein, I will combine all my wishes into one for both of you. May you be as happy with your husband as I was with your grandfather. Renilein, you saw our marriage. Strive to have one like it.

A woman must be smart and never forget that the man stands above her and most of the time can have the last word. Remember that, my Renichen. Then your marriage will be a happy one. After all, it isn't difficult for a woman to submit to the man she loves. Certainly a man must also give in to the woman. They must complement each other. Both of you must always remember that. Then your marriage will have the happiness that I implore God to grant you.

Renchen, another request to you. My mother always said, "When a daughter gets married, one gains a son." Renilein, see that Egon is a good son to your mother. Don't forget her.

I don't have to tell you, my child, how I feel writing this letter. But one has to keep a stiff upper lip. We cannot change anything.

And so, I wish all of you a wonderful celebration. May this day be a beautiful memory for you. I know that all of you will think of me, as all my thoughts will be with you.

My dear ones, all of you, I embrace you warmly and am always,

Your Mother and Grandmother, Jenny, who loves you all.

August 28, 1940

My beloved good Ernilein,

Now you have a married daughter and I want to wish for you that they will be happy, but that in their happiness they will not forget you. And, especially, that they will not make you a grandmother too soon.

I had a little get-together here on the occasion of the wedding, thanks to the coffee you sent. It was very nice. Mille and her husband were extremely nice. In addition to a decorated table, there were gifts for me, and a real wedding meal, with wine, etc. It was marvelous. Mr. Aufrecht proposed a toast. I did not expect that from him.

I am surprised that you did not get a letter from Kurt; he even sent me a copy of his letter of congratulations to you. Has it arrived by now? He is not doing too well; his wife is probably in Cologne already. . . .

Ernilein, you really made me very happy with the coffee you sent me. You wouldn't believe how badly we need it sometimes. But I only have it every Sunday and on special occasions like the 25th [my wedding day]. I am rationing it very carefully. You do not have to send me any butter for now. I have enough for the time being. If I need anything I will write. It is now possible to get packages from the Netherlands.

How I would like to be with you, my child, then you would not feel so lost, and I would be glad to be of help to you. But, Ernilein, we will have to give up that hope.

You will have to tell me in detail about the wedding. You can imagine that I want to know everything.

Now, my Ernilein, that is almost all for today. Only one more thing: Paula's birthday is on the 12th of September. Do not forget it. Sigmund's birthday was yesterday. Tony was also here on Sunday.

Greetings and kisses to you all.

Your very loving Mother

September 17, 1940

My dear Ruth,

I was very happy that you have finally decided to allow yourself a few days of vacation. I can see from the little snapshot that it agreed with you. There really is no point in wearing yourself out completely. One day you just won't be able to go on. So please, from now on, some moderation.

Our dear Jenny is with us now, and we will do our very best to take care of her. She will probably tell you that she is quite satisfied with the change. What she wishes for most, of course, is to be with you. Well, with God's help that will happen, too. Never give up hope or lose faith. I understand that your dear son is giving you much pleasure, too. Let's hope that it'll always be so.

Now, my dear Ruth, my husband and I want to wish you all the best for your birthday and to you and all your loved ones everything good for the coming Rosh Hashanah. Whatever else there is to report you hear from your dear mother, who certainly is an ardent letter writer.

Again, all the best. My husband sends his best regards, too.

In old friendship,

Yours,
Mille Aufrecht

October 2, 1940 [Rosh Hashanah]

My beloved good children,

After no news from you for the past three weeks, I received four pieces of mail, the last one with pictures, which made me incredibly happy. I can see how happy you all are. Only Stepp is so serious. It is sad that the boy has such an unhappy childhood. Renilein, in comparison, you had it 100 percent better. Who would have thought that he would have to earn money at such a young age? But maybe he will be rewarded for it in later years.

Tonight another year has passed for us. I am not going to Temple; instead, I will pray at home. And, as always, I will pray to God that all of you may be happy, healthy and content, and that, if it is meant to be, we can celebrate together next year.

It is now nine in the morning. I am taking this letter to the post office and then I am going to Weissensee [Cemetery]. I can only envy Vati again.

I cannot tell you how happy the pictures make me, Renilein. I recognize the china and the candle sticks, and I see your beaming faces, and I have only the one wish to see you that happy always. Ernilein, you and Ruth look amazingly alike in the picture. I never noticed before how much!

My regards to Ruth and Steve. I will write to them again on Saturday.

Now, my loved ones, take care. I greet you and kiss you all.

Your always loving Mother

October 1940

Renilein, your letter to Marianne arrived in time for her birthday. She was very happy about it.

It makes me very glad, Renilein, that you are so happy with Egon. Hold on to this happiness; there is nothing better in life than husband and wife.

Here I am only the cook, without pay. Everything tastes wonderful, and Mr. Adolf (Aufrecht) says that I do not have to be afraid of losing my job. I can imagine! Everyone would like to have such an inexpensive servant. On holidays Mille goes to Temple and then comes home and sits down at a set table.

Other than that, I don't have anything to tell you today, I think I have chatted enough.

Take care, my Renilein.

Your always loving Grandmother.

Give my warm regards to Egon, as well as to Mutti, Ruth, and Stepp.

October 29, 1940

My beloved Children,

Your letter of the 14th arrived yesterday, Ernilein, and I am very happy that you are doing well. I only hope to get such news many more times. You do not have to send me tea, Ernilein. Ruthelein, I have had no news from you yet, but I hope to get it soon. I can imagine how hopeless Claire's letter to you was. If you saw her, you would be speechless; she looks like a ghost. This week she was especially upset, because she lost all the food stamps she had just received, so now she will not get groceries for the whole month. Of course, we all have to give her some of ours. She really gets terribly mixed up.

Yesterday I visited Toni, who was sick for two weeks. I am supposed to send you her best.

We already had frost last night, and now it is 4 degrees Celcius. I am afraid of another winter.

All of us have given up hope of joining you, *but we will surely go on a journey.* It is probably only a question of time now. We have resigned ourselves to that fact. Whatever happens, my dearest ones, don't worry. I will bear life the way it comes. Our fate is sealed. I had only hoped for a different end to my life and many others along with me. I was lucky to have had a good husband, good children, and much beauty in my life. Now I have to accept the less than pleasant ending, whichever way it happens.

My beloved ones, I have to stop now. The letter has to go to the post office. Take care, I kiss you and hug you.

Your faithful, loving Mother

Friday, December 27, 1940

My beloved, good children,

I have just come from Else's [a friend] and am still completely mixed-up. She is doing very badly. She is not allowed to work, she cannot ride on a train because she cannot stand any kind of sudden motion, she cannot bend over, so, in other words, it's a life where death would be better. It is terrible, a person who is only fifty-two years old!

From Else's, I went to the customs office to pick up a package from Kurt. I was speechless! He sent me coffee, tea, cocoa, cheese, chocolate, cookies, peas, oatmeal, sausage, and two cans of milk! What do you say to that? I am very grateful for his thoughtfulness and I will thank him tomorrow. I was happiest about the milk, which I miss very much.

It has now been four weeks since I have had a letter from you and, even if it is no consolation, I am comforted by the fact that others have not received any mail either.

I spent Christmas very quietly. On the first day I was alone, on the second day we played bridge. Now the old year is almost over, we know the sadness which lies behind us. May the new year bring us some happiness. Foremost, I have one wish, to be united with all of you once more, and may God grant you contentment, health, and happiness.

Ruthelein, when are you going to become an American? It must be almost five years that you are there.

My affidavit expires in February. What will happen without Arne? It is probably better to wait with the renewal, so that it does not have to be renewed again next year.

Ernilein, I have not heard from any of your friends. You know, one is easily forgotten. Everyone has so many things of their own on their mind. Everyone has their own worries. And everyone thinks that they are suffering the most.

Have you heard anything from Arne?

Renilein, how are you? You write to me so rarely. So quickly one forgets those who are far away. But I will never forget any of you. I think of you from morning till night.

Now, my beloved ones, once again, take care. I wish you the best for the New Year.

> With love, your Mother
>
> *Saturday, January 11, 1941*

My beloved, good children,

. . . I don't know if you received my letters, and you must be worried if you did not get any mail. Unfortunately, I cannot take this worry from you. One doesn't even know why the mail is not getting through.

Can you get really nice lace there? Is it expensive? Or is there no interest in that? Please answer these questions for me. [She was obviously thinking of bringing some lace to sell here so that we would have some money. Many of the refugees brought things for that purpose.]

Mille will soon have to give up several rooms. It will not be as nice as it has been until now, but we have to cope with that, too. Aunt Paula has already rented out two rooms, and she will probably rent one more.

What I witness between the "married couple" is unbelievable and especially unpleasant for me. I am standing between the "tree and its bark." They have been married for forty-one years and can't get along. Both are to blame. [It was very unpleasant for her to witness the constant fighting and bickering of the Aufrechts.] This is only meant for you. I now see more and more what kind of a husband I had. But it's all over.

In the next few days I will visit Mathilde [a friend] again. I got a card from Betty this week, and also a package with cheese, cream cheese, and Liptauer cheese which I shared with the Ebensteins. Bernhard [Betty's husband] writes that business is becoming more difficult every day and that they have a lot of worries. Jenny Frohmann does not write at all. I assume that she is busy and can't think about anything. I can understand all that; one slowly becomes egotistical. I only think of you and want news about your well-being; I am not interested in anything else.

Now, my loved ones, there is nothing else to tell you today. I greet and kiss you heartily.

Your very loving Mother

February 12, 1941

My beloved Ernilein,

Today I am writing to answer your question regarding your possible marriage. Ernilein, I don't have to tell you how happy it would make me to know that you are taken care of. Ernchen, I am an old woman, and I see how sad it is to be alone, being the fifth wheel everywhere. Therefore, my child, I can only tell you: don't think it over so long if you like the man and are convinced that you'll have a good life with him. Above all, you write that he is somewhat Vati's type. If so, I say to you, marry him!

Ernchen, you know that it has always been a great worry for me to know that you are so alone. You are getting older, my child, and to be dependent on Reni some day is not such a great prospect. If you have a husband at your side who cares about you, it's a different story. Therefore, Ernilein, I beg you, marry him. Ruth also wrote nice things about him and, after all, neither of you are children any longer and know a little about how to judge people. I hope you will soon make me happy with the news, "I am getting married." We don't have too much pleasant news anymore.

Today I received another package from Kurt. Isn't that touching? It certainly helps me a lot, and I cannot thank him enough. But he wrote that it probably will have to end soon. [Mail from the Netherlands was no longer going to go through.] Betty has already written the same thing. If I could only talk to you for one hour. . . .

Kurt writes that he is terribly worried about Hanna [his sister]. Fritz [Kurt's brother] wrote that Hanna is very sick. She does not write to him. He wants to know if I have heard anything, but I know nothing. Erich [Kurt's cousin] wrote to thank me for sending him your letter. They were very happy to hear from you. Mrs. Heller wrote that they finally got their visa and are leaving in a few days. She asked for your address. I asked her to come to see me once more, but received no reply. . . .

The *Hilfsverein* [a Jewish organization which helped with immigration and other details] is now working with the Consulate in high gear, and people say that things are supposed to become a little easier. I also heard that a Jewish organization in the United States has made· 1500 passages available. Maybe you can find out about that. I would be so happy if I could come to you. . . .

I will answer Reni's letter shortly. Ernilein, please see to it that she writes a nice letter to her father. After all, it won't do her any harm if she asks him to forget what happened before your departure. I'm begging you to do this. I understand that he is suffering because of this situation.

Now, my Ernilein, I ask you again: If you like the man, don't hesitate so long. It would make me very happy to know that you are happy.

Give my fond regards to Ruth as well as to Stevie. To you, my child, a kiss and a warm embrace.

From your mother, who loves you very much and thinks about you all the time.

February 20, 1941 [incomplete]

My beloved good children,

Today I received your letters of January 23 from Erna, Ruth, and Reni, and I was so happy to hear from all of you. In the meantime, I hope you, Ernilein, have set a date for your wedding. I don't have to tell you how happy it makes me to know that you will have someone at your side who will be there for you. You will soon get used to having someone walk beside you, and you'll be glad to know where you belong. Now, Ernilein, you have to be smart and learn to adapt and accommodate. I ask you strongly to do so!

Aunt Paula was here when your letters arrived. I feel so sorry for her. She has lost fourteen pounds in three weeks. She imagines that Alfred [her son] is dead. Therefore, I beg you, please try to find out something about him. It has to be possible, especially since he is supposed to be married. Above all, try to get his address and send it.

Renerchen, you don't know how happy I was about your letter. With regard to Marianne . . . I don't agree with her plan [to marry an American in order to go there]. She could have great difficulties in pursuing it. Her parents are not in agreement, either. After all, the man is forty years old, twenty years older than she. But everyone is enormously impressed by your offer of help. So am I, my child.

Ruthelein, I am reading your letter with very mixed feelings. I ask myself how we deserved this fate. But I suppose there is no use asking this question! Ruthelchen, many parents are getting out now whose numbers are higher than mine. Their children are sending the passage and affidavits. [We left no stone unturned trying to raise the money but we simply were unable to do so.] The *Hilfsverein* asked again if they should wire you. [End of letter]

March 1, 1941

My beloved Renilein,

This is the second time I have to wish you a "Happy Birthday" by mail. This time, my child, it's a special date. Twenty years old as a married woman. Renerle, can you imagine that on a day like this I'm thinking of you more than on any other day? The wishes I'm asking God to grant you are health, contentment, and happiness in your marriage and in all the things you endeavor. I hope your life will be everything you wish for yourself. Then nothing will be missing.

Your letter of January 1 arrived only today. I think it is just wonderful that you wrote to Mrs. Roosevelt on my behalf. [I appealed to Eleanor Roosevelt for help in getting my grandmother over here—to no avail.] Unfortunately, nothing will help. We'll just have to wait. Maybe we'll see each other once more, my child. I have no other wish. Only God knows if it will be fulfilled. In the meantime, you probably got my letter regarding the *Hilfsverein*, and I hope I get an answer from you very soon.

I was very happy to hear your report about your job. I know you are very efficient, and your superiors are always satisfied with your work. It must be a very nice feeling for you.

I've written to your father several times about you, and he promised to write to you. I'm surprised that he has not done so by now. I also haven't heard from him for quite a while. I'm waiting with anticipation for an answer regarding the affair Schrijver [a business deal involving my father and grandfather from years ago].

Renilein, please take care of Stevie. Be nice to him. I'm so sorry for him because I know how attached he is to his father, and he will miss him terribly now that he has left the country. [He had to leave because he was addicted to drugs and the narcotics agents were after him.]

Now, my dearest Renilein, I wish you for your new year, once again, everything good. Have a nice birthday and think of me. Many regards and kisses for you and Egon.

Your Grandmother who loves you very much.

March 1, 1941

My dearest Children,

Today, even more than ever, I have the need to talk to you. It's Vati's birthday. Tomorrow I'm going to the cemetery.

This morning a letter arrived from you, Ruthelein, dated February 3. The content, unfortunately, does not make me very happy because I see that you are going to quit your job, and I can certainly understand it. You cannot continue to let those women [board members of the convalescent home where she works] torture you. I hope that God will send them a fate like yours, so that they will know what they are doing.

Ruthelein, Lily [Mille Aufrecht's sister] would also like to start a business. Maybe you can open a knitting store together. Pepi [the Aufrechts' son] certainly will know where you can reach her. Maybe you will get in touch with her.

Ernilein, I'm still waiting for a telegram from you—until today, unfortunately, in vain. Is the decision that difficult for you, my child? Why don't you take life in a little lighter vein? Believe me, you will be happier when you have somebody at your side who will take care of you. I am sure you will soon see that there is only husband and wife. Of course, you must respect and like the man, too. Everything will work itself out in a marriage. Only, Ernilein, don't hesitate so long.

On Monday I'm going to have more company for coffee. Toni has been away for the past three weeks.

On Wednesday, Mille will be sixty years old. Unfortunately, she does not have an easy life with that man. He's a very difficult person, extremely conceited—even today. He still thinks he is God and that everybody has to dance when he whistles. He's very nice to me, but I feel so sorry for Mille.

I greet you and kiss you, my dearest one.

And I'm always your mother, who loves you

March, 1941

My dearest Renerchen,

I imagine that I can still call you that even if you are already an old married woman. I suppose I should have written you a really big letter and not a little thin piece of paper that is only attached to your grandmother's letter. But at the moment I'm really very busy and I don't have much time to write long letters. But you know that I love you and always wish you the best that you can have.

Stay well and I hope that God will fulfill all your wishes. I hope that is the best thing I can tell you. I hope that you will always be happy and content.

My husband and I wish you the best with all our hearts. Anything else that's going on you hear from your dear grandmother, and I don't have to add anything.

Please give our regards to your husband and all your loved ones. Have a nice day on your birthday. Be happy and best regards from me and my husband. I'm sending you a big birthday kiss in old friendship and love.

Mille Aufrecht

March 8, 1941

My dearest beloved children,

I haven't heard from you for the past two weeks, and I'm waiting for news more than ever. I really would like to know what happened to Alfred. His parents keep asking me questions because they think I know something about him. It is terrible to live with such uncertainty. He's been gone almost four months now and hasn't written a single letter to his parents. It's not understandable. Finally, one must have some certainty. He cannot have disappeared from this earth. You absolutely have to find out what happened. You can't even recognize his mother anymore.

I have not heard from Kurt and Jenny for a while, nor from Betty, either. I have no idea what's going to happen to them. Maybe you will hear from them. [These people are my father and a friend and my cousins who lived in Amsterdam, and this must have been the period when Germany was preparing to occupy the Netherlands and communication to the outside world was difficult.]

Today I heard that Pepi [Mille's son] was drafted into the American army. Not so great for his young wife. But he's happy about it for many reasons. I hope that Egon doesn't have to go, as well.

Ernilein, I'm really surprised that I still haven't heard anything definite about you. When are you going to make a decision?

Herta comes to visit me more often now. I met Willi today and he told me that his work is very hard. He has slimmed down considerably. Yes, our life is not very easy right now. I'm only happy that I know you are there. You hit the jackpot. You cannot thank Ruth and Arnold enough for making it possible for you to get there. I never imagined it would be so difficult for me, however.

Ernilein, if you should go to New York sometime, please see if you can find Mrs. Frankenstein [a former neighbor]. She has so many friends and acquaintances, maybe someone will do something for me there. They are not going to run any risks.

Now, my dear ones, I want to close. I must take the letter to the post office. Farewell. I greet you and kiss you and I'm always

Your mother who loves you.

March 12, 1941

My dearest Ruthelein,

I just came back from playing bridge with Mrs. Hirsch [a friend] and found your letter of February 16th. Ruthelchen, why are you still so unhappy? It makes me very sad when I see how you suffer. I understand you, my child, like nobody else. But I still have to tell you, don't take it so hard. I'm sure that for you the sun will shine again. What you are going through with Arne is certainly not happening unexpectedly. One was always prepared for such an end. But it is not right for him to make your life so difficult with his letters. You cannot help him any longer. He has to know this now, once and for all. Ruthelchen, the sixteen years you lived with him really wore you out enough. You know that I love him very, very much, but you really have to free yourself now. It's very difficult for me, my child, to write this to you. However, there is no other way out. [His drug addiction finally caught up with him. Being a physician, he was able to write so many prescriptions for himself that the narcotics agents were after him. They were convinced that he was peddling drugs, and he had to leave the United States to escape being arrested.]

Ruthelchen, if I could only come to you. If you could make a home for yourself, how gladly would I cook and help you in any way I could. But I have no hope regarding my coming to you. Bringing something, my child, is unfortunately not the way you imagine. Now I can take only 100 pounds of luggage, so if I take my personal things— underwear and clothing—it is already 100 pounds.

Today I had a very nice letter from Paula Hirschkorn [a friend]. She writes that you are angry at her because she wrote that she cannot give an affidavit for me. She said there's no one she would rather have done it for, but unfortunately she can't do it. Otherwise she would certainly have done it for her siblings, and they are all still here, too.

Tomorrow is Stevie's birthday and Clare asked me to come for coffee tomorrow afternoon. I also had a very nice letter from Else [a relative of Arnold]. She is working for a Jewish organization, and Clare hopes she can do something for her.

Ruthelchen, you have to send me a letter right away that I can show to the *Hilfsverein*, to the effect that you cannot send me the entire passage, that you can pay only about $200 and that you hope I can pay something for the passage from the money I still have. And if that is not possible, you can still try to pay it from there. If it were only possible that I could come to you, my happiness would be complete. You can't imagine what is going on here. I'm only living with the thought about you. I would be satisfied with everything. I would not ask for anything.

I would only help you as far as my strength holds out.

Antonia has been away for five weeks and is expected back in the next few days. I'm going to see her right away.

I cannot understand why Erna is hesitating so long about her marriage. There's an old proverb that says, if the bride hesitates too long, then the bridegroom thinks it over, too. I would be so happy if I knew she was being taken care of.

Steppke, I thank you for your letter. I was very happy to get it. I put some new stamps on my last letter to you, but there have been no new ones out since then. [Steve has been a stamp collector since those early days. He has published stamp catalogs and written stamp columns for various publications, including the *Cleveland Plain Dealer*. He's also a stamp trader.]

Now, my dear ones, farewell.

I greet you and kiss you both and I am, with love,

Your Mother

March 14, 1941

My dearest Children,

. . . Renilein, I thank you so much for your dear letter. You've really made me very happy. Please don't start a fight over me about where I'm going to live when I come over there. I only wish it were not so far off. To go to the Consulate is useless because everything now goes through the *Hilfsverein*. As soon as I know something more, I'll write to you. And I have to have a new affidavit.

I had another visitor, a Mrs. Silz [an acquaintance]. She's almost eighty years old, but her mind is like that of a thirty-year-old. She has also given up her apartment and lives with somebody else. Very sad.

Renilein, I imagine that Marianne has already written to you that her marriage plans are not working out the way she thought. Her father consulted a lawyer with her, and he told her all the difficulties and eventualities and that is why she's not going to go through with it.

I had a letter from Jenny today after a very long time. It was not very happy. She also wrote to you, Renilein, at the time of your birthday. I hope your father also remembered your twentieth birthday.

I cooked dinner today and wish that you could have seen how Mille and Adolf enjoyed it. He said he would like to "retire" his maid so that I could cook all the time. But thank you very much, I wouldn't like to do it on a steady basis.

Now, my dear ones, all of you, farewell. I have to take these letters to the post office. I greet you and kiss you, and I am, as always,

Your loving Mother

March 18, 1941

My dearest Children,

Today I got your telegram and I thank you very much. At first, I thought it was news that you, Ernilein, got married. But I can see that you're still not sure. Tomorrow I'll take the telegram to the *Hilfsverein* to hear if there is any hope of getting [a visa] outside the quota! At the moment, you cannot do it via Lisbon, either. The only way is via Moscow, and that takes six weeks. But I would even do that if I could just come to you. Well, we'll wait.

A few days ago I had a letter from Linchen in Amsterdam. She writes that Kurt's wife went to Cologne, and Kurt is having his meals at her house. Well, I suppose this marriage is going to break up also. So he will be alone in his old age, as well. Strangely enough, I have not received any answers from him to my various letters, and I'm really waiting for news from him.

On March 13, Clare gave a tea in honor of Stevie's birthday, and I will do the same on the 24th for you, Renilein. I invited my friends, but one of them told me that Clare said she was not going to come because I only invited her for Reni's birthday. And Arne, after all, had a birthday also. [My uncle's birthday was on the same day.] I should have said that. What do you think of such foolishness?

Herta came to visit me today, too. She is very, very tired and very weak. She's working a lot. Her mother can do more than she does. Willi [her husband] leaves for work at 1:30, Marianne in the morning at 5:30, and Bobby [Marianne's brother] at 8:00. Everybody eats at a different time. . . . It's very difficult.

Clare thinks Arne will do the same as his Uncle Meyers did, and someday he might have to do it. ["It" refers to committing suicide, because of Arne's long-time drug addiction.] I can't even think of it. Such a wonderful man ruined his life like that.

Otherwise, my dear ones, there is nothing more to tell today and I greet you and kiss you warmly.

Your loving Mother

April 8, 1941

My dearest Children,

I got your telegram on Saturday and I'm so sorry that you have to spend so much money for me, but it is the only possible way to reach our goal.

Ernilein, I wrote to you that I went to see the relatives of Mrs. Levy, but I did not find them at home. So they came to see me on

Sunday. They are fine. They have written to Mrs. Levy and were surprised that they didn't get an answer. The most important thing for me is that the uncle is very well versed in all the intricacies of emigration, and he offered to do everything for me. I'm very grateful because I cannot do all this by myself.

Yesterday I was at the Hapag [a shipping company] with Mr. M. [an acquaintance] and in the meantime you probably have received the telegram from there and answered me regarding that. I hope you have paid the money at the Joint Distribution Committee. After you have taken care of everything over there, including affidavits with tax reports, and all the required papers, only then can one go to the Consulate here. And then they're going to take care of the passage. The man at the *Hilfsverein* told me you should ask for Form 575 from Washington. That is regarding privileged status for parents. Then I might be able to get away in July or August.

I can't even imagine such happiness. Unfortunately, Arnold is no longer there for the affidavit. But the man asked that you especially state that you've been there for four years. Besides that, Ernilein, you probably got married in the meantime and perhaps your husband will also give an affidavit for me as well as Egon. With God's help I certainly won't burden any of you. On the contrary, I hope to be of help to you. I only would like to come to you as soon as possible.

Paula is a little calmer now since Alfred sent a telegram. But I still cannot understand why no letter has come from him since February 6. His new wife could have written as well.

Marianne is coming to visit me on the holidays with a young friend who is going to Boston at the beginning of May. Herta told me that this young girl will have a big position there. I will send you her name. Marianne and Herta visit me quite often now. A friend wrote an affidavit for Marianne, and she would be very happy to get out together with me.

In May, Mrs. Bernstein [Marianne's voice teacher] is going to give a song recital in Herta's apartment, and I will finally hear Marianne sing. I'm really looking forward to hearing some music again.

I'm very happy that I gave up my apartment. Paula and Mille have only one room now, too. Everything works out if one is willing. The most important thing is to live together with congenial people. I hear very little from Amsterdam now.

Otherwise, my dearest ones, farewell. I greet you and kiss you.

As always, your loving Mother

April 23, 1941

My dearest Ernilein,

. . . As soon as I have a new affidavit and a certificate that the passage has been paid for, I will certainly try to get away from here as fast as possible. The biggest difficulty really is regarding the passage. Ernilein, please write to Alfred that he should also try to send an affidavit for his parents. He should get in touch with friends to give additional affidavits. And he should also write to his parents that he can pay part of the passage. He has to do this very quickly because his mother is really desperate, and I wouldn't be surprised if one day she ends it all! She doesn't even believe that he wrote at all because everyone else gets letters. Why should his letters always get lost?

I had a lot of company today. Marianne, Herta, Betty Rothschild, and Paula. It was really a little too much for one day, since I visited Toni in the morning as well.

I was very happy to hear that the relatives are willing, so quickly, to help with the passage money for me. Please thank them in my name. I will also write to Kansas City. Maybe they will also help, so it won't be so difficult for you. It would be awful if the $400 for the passage got lost. It would be unthinkable.

Now I have something very difficult ahead of me. I have to have seven teeth extracted. I'm so afraid of that. But then those teeth won't bother me anymore.

Marianne can't wait to get her affidavit. She hopes to leave together with me. I would be very happy about that.

I'm glad that Stevie is such a nice child. When he gets older, he'll probably calm down somewhat. Unfortunately, he has inherited the nonstop talking from his other grandmother.

It's going to be very difficult for me here from now on. On the first of May our maid is leaving, and I will probably have to cook and do a lot of other things because Mille doesn't know anything about housework. I certainly don't like it very much, but what else can I do? I'm not going to work too hard because the "man of the house" will ask for everything from us the way it was before, and Mille thinks he will ask for even more. He can't stand to see anybody sitting down. He always wants something. I see again and again what a wonderful husband I had. [Mr. Aufrecht was obviously a tyrant, who expected everyone to cater to him. When the maid left, my grandmother helped out a great deal.]

Now, my dearest one, I'm closing for today. On Saturday I'll write to Ruth. Give her my best regards.

I greet you and kiss you and embrace you.

Always, your loving Mother

May 5, 1941

My beloved Renerchen,

I received your letter today and hope that you are used to being alone with your husband and that you don't miss Mutti too much. But now you have a replacement—Aunt Ruth and Steve. I hope you are all getting along well. [After my marriage, my mother lived with us at first and, after her marriage, my aunt and my cousin moved in with us.]

You can imagine that I worry about Aunt Ruth a lot. I hope she will find a good job very quickly. I also pictured her life a little differently, but that is fate, I suppose.

Renilein, I don't believe I will get away in August if you're unable to book a passage for me. I went to the *Hilfsverein* today to get my certificate for this booking. But I can't get it right now, and without it I can't get a passage. So you see, the prospects aren't too good, though I want to come to you so badly. *I'm happy that at least you got away. Renilein, you would be very unhappy here.*

I haven't heard from Marianne for quite a while. She's also very anxious to leave. She thinks that once she has an affidavit she will get away, but, unfortunately, it's very difficult. There is so much red tape.

Your father sent me a copy of his letter to you, and I was very happy to hear about it, as I'm sure you were, too. It was very nice that he sent Egon his watch [gift from my grandparents on the occasion of my parents' wedding]. I hope it will arrive soon. It's very valuable and cost a lot. [My husband was very happy with that gift and he cherished the watch for many years].

Renilein, I would be grateful if you could write me a little more about Mutti's husband. I don't know anything about him—what he does, what he is like. Do you like him? Are you and Egon getting along with him? As you can imagine, Renerchen, I want to know everything that is happening in your lives.

Renilein, it makes me very happy that you are such a good housewife. Believe me, my child, it is very nice when a girl is a good housekeeper and has a clean house. Even if we argued sometimes about trifles, it was beautiful when we were together, and now it's very sad to be so alone.

Now, my Renerle, I have to close. I have to be at the dentist's at ten o'clock. He really tortures me.

So long, my Renerlein. I hug you and kiss you and Egon, and I am, as always,

Your loving Grandmother

May 16, 1941

My dearest Ernilein,

Today I got your letter of April 18 in which you write that you're going to be married on April 30. I assume that this is now a fact, and I want to wish all the best to you and your husband for your marriage. Ernilein, you know what I wish for you. All my wishes are together in this one wish, that I hope you will be lucky enough to find happiness at the side of your husband, like the happiness I had for twenty-seven years. I'm not worried about your marriage. You are both old enough to know what's important in a marriage. One has to have consideration and regard for the other, and everything has to be said calmly and peacefully until you become accustomed to each other.

Yesterday the affidavits arrived. I thank you very much. I'm having them copied today and will send them to the Consulate as soon as I have them. Everything is very difficult. When you have one item, then you're missing another. And there's an awful lot of running around. You know what it means, Ernilein, but it's much worse today than it was two years ago.

Please, my child, write to me, and let me know everything about how your life is now going to be. Wasn't it hard for Reni to part with you? I imagine that the letter from Kurt got to Reni in the meantime. He sent it on March 22 and sent me a copy. I told him that he sent the birthday letter quite late. But I'm sure that Reni will be very happy to get it, just the same.

Ruth is writing so little now that I'm worried about her. I hope I'll get a long letter very soon. I'm glad I no longer have an apartment. Aunt Paula has rented out four rooms. There are seven people in the apartment. Paula would also rather give it up. All they have left is their bedroom.

Marianne just came to visit me, and I'm always very happy to see her. She did send a telegram to Reni regarding an affidavit. I hope she will be able to come to you. [She never made it; she was murdered in Auschwitz].

Now, my Ernilein, farewell. Give my regards to your husband. I will be very happy to get a picture from you and also a few words from him. To you, my child, my best regards and kisses from your loving mother. Best regards to Ruth, Stevie, Reni, and Egon.

Your loving Mother

May 20, 1941

My dearest Ruthelchen,

I got your letter of April 29 today and learned that you're finally going to give up your job. It's probably for the best. I know how hard you worked, my child, but you will find something else. Can't Herta help you to start a little business of your own, as you thought you might? I'm sure her husband has plenty of money. Also, he does have a travel agency. Couldn't he get a passage for me? Maybe you'll get in touch with him once more. I would just love to be with you, Ruthelchen. You can't imagine.

Now, there's another document I need that I don't have. Who knows how long I'll have to wait for that?

Ruthelchen, I'm very happy that Erna is married and I only hope it will be all right and that they will be happy. Who would ever have thought that I would be alive and not be with you at Reni and Erna's marriages? I would bear everything if I could only be sure of coming to you soon. Believe me, my child, the problems are overwhelming.

Aunt Paula just left. I feel so sorry for her. She is suffering so much because of the lack of communication from her son. Can you imagine, since the 20th of November they have received one letter, and it said nothing. Not that he was married, nothing about his life, there was just nothing. Only that he doesn't like it there [California]. The climate doesn't agree with him, and he will probably go somewhere else. And that's all. No pictures, nothing. It is really unheard of. His wife could have written a few words, too.

Clare was here again today. She is very upset that you paid the passage for me. "And what's going to happen to me?" she asked. What shall I answer her? I'm surprised that Arne writes so little. I don't believe that he will forget you. But maybe that would be the best for you, my child. Because as sad as it is, you will not get together again. Ruthelchen, I don't even want to think that he might have a very sad end.

We really seem to have bad luck. But, my child, the "old" God is still alive. Maybe some day it will be different for you, too. Let's hope for that. Don't give up, Ruthelchen. I feel so sorry for Stevie. I know how much he loves his father.

Ruthelchen, isn't it a little strange for Reni to be without her mother? But it's probably the best for everyone concerned. Please give her my regards. The next letter is for her. I'm really happy that she's so worried about me. Maybe she will be able to get a passage for me, so that I might still come to you this year.

I just received your letter of May 3, unbelievably fast! I was very happy to get your account of the wedding and also about Martin's note. I will write to him soon. I'm very glad that Erna now knows where she belongs, and I would be very happy, my child, if I knew the same thing about you.

You know how beautiful my life was in the past, but I have many problems now, and old age and the longing for you. Ruthelein, whatever happened, I had all of you. But now I'm so lonesome. Even if *everybody* is nice to me when I'm sick or something is bothering me, I'm alone after all. Mille is very good, but I don't want to take advantage of her too much because she has enough to do herself. That's why I would like to come to you so badly. At the moment, I have a lot of problems with my teeth.

The next letter is going to Reni and Erna. Please give everyone my regards. I don't have anything more to tell you today, Ruthelchen, and I greet you and Stevie and send you kisses.

Your loving Mother

May 28, 1941

My dearest Ruthelchen,

. . . Yesterday I went to the *Hilfsverein* again. The man who was working on my case until now has left. They asked me to see someone else on Thursday morning, but it will be very difficult if you don't get a passage for me. It's probably going to take a very long time until I can be with you. You can imagine how unhappy I am about that. Believe me, my child, it is no joy to live with somebody else and be dependent on someone else's moods. But what can one do? The thought of seeing you once more keeps me going. Mille is very good to me, but everything has to go the way she wants it, not to speak about him [Mille's demanding husband] at all! . . .

I have difficult days behind me. My teeth gave me a lot of pain, but now they are all out.

Now, my child, I want to close. I greet you and Stevie warmly and am—lovingly—always,

Your Mother

June 6, 1941

My dearest Ernilein,

I haven't heard from you for two weeks, and I haven't had a letter from Ruth for a very long time. But I imagine that this is because she moved. I'm very worried about her.

Thank God that the holidays are past. On such days I miss you even more than usual, and my wish is to be with you on the next holiday. I imagine it will only be possible to come to you when you are able to secure a passage for me. I have very little hope here. At the *Hilfsverein* I was told that I should not expect any kind of news from the Consulate before the end of July. Only then will I get a certificate for a booking. . . . [Seems to be a constant merry-go-round between getting a certificate and booking a passage. If people had one thing, the other was missing. A *Catch-22* situation]. Now we're seven people in the apartment but I'm sure it won't stay that way. It would be awful for me to share a room with a stranger, but that can't be helped either. I'm praying every day that I can come to you soon. . . . My thoughts are with you, all of you, from morning till night. Can you imagine sitting alone all day long in a little room thinking about the past? Then, at four o'clock to go downstairs, having to come back at five o'clock [curfew for Jews]? Sometimes Paula visits and sometimes Mrs. Fuchs [an acquaintance]. But most of the time I'm alone. I had imagined a happier old age.

I just got a letter from your sister-in-law. She said she was going to visit me in the next few days. Otherwise, my child, I have nothing more to report today.

Please give my regards to Ruth, Martin, Reni, Egon, and Stevie.

I greet and kiss you warmly and am as always,

Your loving Mother

June 10, 1941

My dearest beloved children,

Today I got a real shock. I had news from the Consulate that the affidavits are not sufficient. You can imagine how I feel. I don't know if it would be possible for you to put up a $1,000 bond for me. [This bond was obviously required if the affidavit was not deemed to be sufficient, but as I said before, we were unable to raise that kind of money.] You probably got my telegram in the meantime. The news from the Consulate means that I have to have much stronger affidavits and proof of support for my living expenses. [There were four of us working, and we could easily have supported her.] Otherwise, they will not give me a visa.

I was so hopeful, but now I'm down in the dumps again. Who knows if I'm ever going to get out? The accreditation has to be in my name, as you probably know. Maybe the relatives in Brooklyn will do it after all. Or maybe your friend, Herta-Irene. There's no risk for her. After all, her husband is American. That carries a lot of weight. Dear ones, they certainly don't make it easy for us.

Today the Ebensteins had a letter from Alfred. He doesn't mention his wife at all, so they think he isn't even married. It seems that he wants to start a business. He told his parents not to worry. He will get them over there. [He never did; they were deported to Theresienstadt and later to Auschwitz.]

Yesterday a friend of Betty's came to visit me and brought me pictures of Lisa and Helga [daughters of Betty and Bernhardt Meyer, cousins living in Amsterdam] and something for my birthday. It made me very happy. Betty has to work very hard to keep everything going.

I thank you so much for all the birthday wishes. I ask for only one wish, that I can come to you very soon. It would be much easier for all of you, for I would take care of the household chores. Ruthelchen, if you can't handle it any other way, why don't you give your large diamond as collateral for an accreditation for me, and Erna could possibly give them a large rug, or something else. I'm so worried about it. I have only one thought, to come to you as soon as possible. Otherwise, my life has no meaning at all.

Ernilein, should I also learn to fix stockings?

I don't hear anything from Jenny. I told her about your marriage but got no answer to that letter, either.

I have nothing more to tell you today, my dear ones.

I greet you and kiss all of you warmly, and am, as always with love,

Your Mother

June 14, 1941

My dearest children,

Yesterday I got a letter from Egon's brother with a picture. You can't imagine how happy I was with it. Martin looks very nice and is really somewhat the type of Adolf Pelz. I only hope and wish that he will be like him in many ways.

Unfortunately I can't tell you anything good about me. I am very sad. I have to leave my room and live in a little room in the back of the apartment. A couple will take my room. You can imagine how much work this is going to be for me again. Hina is not here, and Mrs. Gottschalk is not here and our maid has left now too. I really don't know what to do anymore.

I will always remember my sixty-seventh birthday. If only I could come to you, but I have no hope anymore. Yesterday, my dentist told me that if you could get a pretty substantial affidavit from an American, you do not need accreditation. I don't know what to believe anymore. If they would only give us proper information at the Consulate, but when they write, they tell you right away that they don't want to hear any questions. If I only could be where Vati is [cemetery], then you would be rid of one more worry, and I would be rid of them all.

Mille has to go into one room with her husband and there will now be five different parties cooking in that small kitchen. I feel very sorry for her. She has to do everything herself now, and it's very hard for her. But we have to live through it as long as we can. She has no help at all from her husband. On the contrary, he asks more of her than he used to ask of their maid.

I will now have to give away most of my things because I wouldn't know where to put them. But I'm used to that already. Mille has nothing left except a bed, a table, and an armoire.

Tomorrow, I'm inviting all my friends to my room because after that I can only have two or three people in my little room. But that's not so terrible, either; we'll have to put up with that, too.

Now, my dearest ones, I hope that you, Ruthelchen, feel at home with Reni by now and that you are enjoying each other and getting along well. Did you find any satisfactory work yet? Up to now, my worry was Erna. And now it is you, my child. Why don't I have a nature like many other mothers who can just put everything out of their minds?

I had a card from Jenny in which she congratulates me on the occasion of your marriage, Ernilein. She's so happy that you made the decision, and she would like to do the same. She said she also wrote you.

How are you, Renilein? Are you getting along all right? Can you do everything by yourself? I'm very happy, my child, that you are "crazy clean" like me! I must say that cleanliness is a great virtue.

Renilein, do you think that your boss would give me an affidavit? Is he an American?

While I was writing this, I received a letter from the *Hilfsverein*. My affidavits were given to them, and I'm to pick them up on Thursday. I can imagine what that means. Maybe this is the last letter that you will be getting from me. If that is so, my dearest, then you stay well all of you, and I wish you all the very, very best.

I heard so many good things today about you, dear Martin, from a Mrs. Striem [Martin Summerfield's relative] that I'm very happy to know that you are Erna's husband.

Renilein, Pepi wrote to his parents that he's going to visit you with his wife [son of the Aufrechts, and a former boyfriend of mine]. In the meantime, he has probably been there.

Now, my dearest, farewell. I greet you and I kiss you warmly, and I'm always,

Your very loving Mother

[Letter from Marianne's mother, a childhood friend of Erna, approximately June 1941]

My dear Ernchen,

I am just visiting your mother and heard, with regret, that you did not hear from me on the occasion of your marriage. I wrote you a long letter in March, and I thought that you would probably get it quickly and on time.

Now I want to repeat my warmest congratulations. I am very happy that you made this decision. May everything be for the best and may it bring you the luck that you have missed for so long. Our best wishes to your dear husband as well.

Next time I will write you in more detail, but today I am in a great rush. Best regards to you and Reni, and your men.

Yours,
Herta

July 1, 1941

My dearest Ruthlein,

I got your letter and hope that you have calmed down a little in the meantime and that you have already had some rest by now.

I'm sure that you can imagine how I feel. I'll probably have to give up all hope of coming to you unless, of course, you can get a visa for me via Washington. I was told that they check the affidavits in Washington to determine whether they are sufficient. If they are, a visa is issued. I am told that there are several Consulate officials at the Embassy there [in Washington] who continue to work on our immigration. [I assume that staff, working on immigration, was curtailed considerably by that time. Congress was trying hard to keep people out of the country, and it proves the well-known documented fact that, under orders from Assistant Secretary Breckenridge Long, who had been chosen by FDR to handle immigration problems, overseas consulates were ordered to "put every obstacle in the way of processing visas." Half of the immigration slots for Europeans went unused during the Nazi era!] Mr. Miller wanted to send a telegram via the Hapag, but I think it's really pointless because I can't tell you everything so clearly in a telegram. Maybe you can contact Senator Lodge once more. [Massachusetts senator, who was known to try to help in immigration matters]. I don't know if there's any point to it, but anyway I'm writing to beg you not to leave a stone unturned.

Yesterday I met Mrs. Lachman [an acquaintance] at the *Hilfsverein*. She got passage from over there. She already has a visa and is leaving in the next few days. Her sister and brother-in-law left about eight weeks ago. Yes, there are some lucky people!

I hope that this letter reaches you because I have been without news from you for the last two weeks. I hope to hear from you very soon. Your letters are my only joy.

On the 15th I'm going to change my room, not very nice, but it can't be helped. We have to resign ourselves to everything.

Today I had a visit from Erna Babb [a friend and confidante]. She came here from her garden. It was very nice. When the weather is better, I'm going to go out there one day, but at the moment it's been raining every day from morning til night. I had a letter from Kurt yesterday. You have probably heard from him in the meantime, too.

Ruthelein, I would be very happy to hear real soon that you have found a good job. Are you living comfortably with Reni and Egon? How does Stevie feel being there? Do you visit Erna often? And how is it going with her? Do you at least have some kind of help from Erna's husband? You see, my child, how everything burdens me, and I think about you constantly. This is what occupies me day and night.

Mr. Aufrecht always tells me that by having so much company I am "a victim of my popularity." As for Clare, she is a victim of her unpopularity. She really is unbearable now. You can't imagine how she fights with everyone. It's just awful.

Ruthelchen, now I want to close for today. Give my love to Erna, Reni, Martin, Egon and Steve.

And for you, my child, my warmest kisses.

Your very loving Mother.

July 7, 1941

My dearest children,

After a long wait, I got your letter of June 16 today. You probably know that there is no use in doing anything right now because there is no hope for any kind of immigration until the war is over. Take the money back from the Joint Distribution Committee and wait, as I have to wait, too. Ernalein, it is easy to say "keep your chin up," but it is very difficult to do this. Believe me, I am afraid we won't ever see each other again.

Ruthelein, on the 16th of June I remembered very vividly my

departure from Palestine five years ago. What we have gone through since then! But I don't think it was the worst yet. If I had only stayed with you. [My grandmother and my mother were in Palestine twice, once in 1936 and one other time, and each time returned to Berlin against the advice of my aunt and my uncle.] Our maid has left, and I can't do all this work much longer, especially in this enormous heat; cooking, cleaning, shopping. It's certainly too much for one person.

I'm very happy to hear what you write about Stevie. I hope you will be able to get him into a camp, and he will come back more relaxed. Once he goes to high school, the demands made on him will be much greater. The main thing, my child, is that you stay well and Stevie will certainly give you much pleasure in the future.

I have to tell you that Reni is absolutely right. I certainly wouldn't want you to go to work in a factory, either. I can't even think of it, but unfortunately I can't help you anymore. It will probably be difficult for you, too, once you have your own apartment. But I can understand that you want to have your own home. The only thing is that Stevie will be left on his own too much. Alas, he's already used to that. I greet you and kiss you warmly and I'm always,

Your loving Mother

Jenny with Aunt Ruth and Stevie (Gideon) in Palestine, 1935

July 18, 1941

My dearest Renilein,

Your letter of June 24 came yesterday, and I thank you very much. Renilein, it's very easy to say keep your chin up, but I can't tell you how difficult that is. I had hoped to be with you very shortly. But alas, alas.

Renilein, my warmest wishes to you and Egon on your first wedding anniversary. I hope you'll always be happy together, and I'm telling you especially to be quiet even if everything isn't the way you thought it would be. Only if the wife gives in, can a marriage be happy.

I cannot agree with you concerning Aunt Ruth. It would be suicide if she were to go back to Arnold. You don't know what she went through in the sixteen years of her marriage. She was nearly a martyr. No other woman would do what she did. Therefore, my child, I beg you, be nice to her and don't make her feel as if she's only being tolerated. Please imagine if Mutti and you had not found a home with us, and you had had to stay in a furnished room with strangers all these years. Would you have had so many beautiful memories of your youth? Didn't I do everything to make you happy? Please do the same for Ruth; you will be doing it for me, too.

I love Arnold very much, and I know that he was there for everybody. But I cannot forgive him for ruining not only the life of my child, but the life of his child as well. He knew what was the matter with him and should not have married. I don't like the affair with the [married] doctor, either; but on the other hand, I can understand that Aunt Ruth would like to have a little happiness. I am praying every day that this affair will end well. So, Renilein, you will fulfill my wish, won't you, my child?

Today it is two years, Reni, since I took you to the train. What have these years brought for me? It is a little too much for a person of my age, and I pray to God every day to fulfill my wish to see all of you once more.

This letter is only for you, my child. Please don't show it to Aunt Ruth.

Now, my child, farewell, and give my best regards to Egon and a warm kiss to you.

Your loving Grandmother

July 25, 1941

My dearest Ruthelchen,

Today I got your letter dated July 8, and I'm happy to see that you are a little more relaxed. I hope that soon you will also find your good mood and sense of humor again.

Erna wrote that I should find out if I can get a visa here without having a ticket. I have written again and again that I first have to have a passage before I can even get a visa. The visa is good only for four months, and I have to have something very definite in my hands. Otherwise, everything starts over from the beginning.

Ruthelchen, I am so desperate that I don't know what to do. Believe me, my child, I would have made an end long ago if I had known for sure that I couldn't come to you. I am not going anywhere else [referring to deportation].

There are five women in the kitchen here now [in the Aufrechts' apartment, which people were forced to share] and, beginning August 1, there will be even more. We're going to have a big family in the dining room. Can you imagine that? I am really sorry for Mille.

Ruthelchen, wouldn't it be better for you right now not to take your own apartment, but to stay with Reni? Isn't it better that you don't burden yourself with an apartment, especially since you are not home all day?

If I could only be there, I would take care of your apartment and do the cooking, etc. Well, maybe you'll still be able to get me over there. Isn't it possible for your friend Herta-Irene to help get a passage for me through her husband's business? I know she would do it for me. She's told me so often how much she likes me. Maybe she can do it.

Ruthelein, you can believe me, I'm not begging you like this for nothing. But first you have to have the information from Washington that the affidavit is sufficient. Then they can work on everything else. But everything must go via Washington. At the *Hilfsverein* they told me that if you no longer have any relatives here, you get out much faster, and I no longer have any.

Ruthelein, what you wrote to me about the doctor makes me feel a little better. You must know yourself if you're not going to have a disappointment, and I pray to God every day that your wish will be fulfilled.

I just had a very nice letter from Kurt. He seems to feel much better. I sent him ten guilder, but he told me not to do this anymore in the future because he's able to send me things out of his own funds. I don't know whether or not his wife is back again. He writes that Fritz [his brother] is asking him to see to it that he can come to America with his son. And he writes that he can't understand why I can't get away—that I was probably wrongly advised by the *Hilfsverein*. Apparently there are different laws in the Netherlands.

I'm glad that Erna and Reni are happy and content. If I only knew that you were happy, too, I would worry a little less about you.

Now, Ruthelein, I have nothing more to tell you today.

I greet you and kiss you and I'm always your mother who loves you very much.

Give my regards to everybody.

August 18, 1941

My dearest Renilein,

Today I want to write a letter to you alone, since Ruth is not living with you anymore. Before, the letters were always meant for both of you. Why did Ruth move out so fast? Couldn't you get along? Maybe it's better this way. I hope there will be peace at Mutti's. Ruth is actually easy to get along with. I feel so sorry for her after she struggled for sixteen years. But I also feel sorry for Arnold. I'm sure it's going to bother him if Ruth divorces him.

Renilein, have you thought very carefully about living with Egon's sister and brother-in-law? Will that work out well?

Four days from now you'll be married one year, my child. I certainly thought that on this day I would already be with you, but now I have given up hope. It looks very sad, and I believe we are not going to see each other again. Renilein, I long for you so much that I don't know what to do, and I can neither sleep nor eat. I use your favorite medicine, Tincture of Valerian. There is not much I can do. I have to live through it.

Ernst [the Aufrechts' son in the U.S.] is said to have a very beautiful apartment, and they seem to be making a good living. Marianne is very sad that there is so little hope of her getting out. Herta won't leave now because she wouldn't leave Bobby [her son] alone, and he can't leave.

I hear very little from your father now. He thanked me very curtly for my birthday congratulations. His wife has obviously not come back, because he wrote that except for his present housekeeper, nobody knew of his birthday. He says he's happy not to see anyone. He just surrounds himself with his dogs because "they're more faithful than people." He must have had some very unhappy experiences.

Aunt Betty wrote that Lisa is not getting married until the war is over. They want to wait and see what's going to happen.

I got two letters from Aunt Ruth this week, dated the 28th and 31st of July. You can't imagine how I always wait for your letters. They are the only thing that still give me pleasure.

On Friday the 15th I went to Weissensee [Cemetery], and when I returned home, Mille told me that Frieda Sonnenschein [our former maid], had been here. She is here on her vacation, and I was sorry to have missed her visit [very courageous of her to visit Jews].

How did you spend your vacation, my child? I imagine it was very nice to have food put in front of you, wasn't it? If I were with you, Renerle, I would be very happy to serve it to you.

Mutti wrote me the other day that she is very happy and content. Can you imagine how happy that makes me?

Now I hope I'll get a long letter from you very soon.

Please give everyone my best regards.

To you, my Renerlein, warmest greetings and kisses.

Your loving Grandmother

August 19, 1941

My dearest children,

Now I am writing to both of you because you are together again. I hope you will get along well and live together in harmony. On Saturday I had a letter from you, Ruthelein, dated July 18, and today a letter dated July 31. I cannot describe how happy I am when I get news from you. That is the only happiness I still have. I am glad, my child, that you are making good money and are happy with your work. I hope that the day will come when you will write that you no longer have to work. I am returning the regards from the doctor.

Your mother-in-law is certainly not all there anymore. We've known this for a long time. One can almost understand that she is so lonesome because she has very few friends. But lately she doesn't want to see anyone, she only wants to be alone. The only one she would like to have with her is her old hairdresser. She gives her everything and informs her about all her affairs as well. You can't talk to her anymore. She says she knows exactly what she's doing. Well, one can't do anything about that.

Ernilein, even if Cuba hadn't been cut off, I certainly wouldn't have gone there anyway because I never would want you to have this kind of burden. You should not go into debt because of me. [It was possible for a long time to have people wait in Cuba until the visa to the U.S. was issued but this door was eventually closed too by the Cuban government]. Now I think that every hope that we will see each other again will have to be forgotten. We also have to be resigned to that, as difficult as it will be. But one gets used to everything. If only I could sleep a little better. It is now two o'clock in the morning, and I can't fall asleep again.

Hina's husband was here yesterday. She has so much work at home that she can hardly come to see me. They are both going to visit their daughter, Ruth. She gave up her job because her boyfriend gives her so much child support that everybody can live on that. She lives near Dresden in the mountains and invited her parents. [Ruth had an illegitimate child with a Jewish man!]

Now, my dearest, I'll close for today. I greet you and kiss you and am always

your loving Mother

August 25, 1941

My dearest children,

I received your letter of August 11, Ruthelein, and I thank you for all the news. If I could only follow your advice not to worry about you, I would feel a little better, but nobody can jump over his own shadow. It makes me very happy to know that you are getting along all right, but I can see from your letters how difficult it is for all of you.

Reni wrote me the other day that she, too, would like to have it a little easier. Couldn't she have waited a few years with this marriage? Wouldn't there have been time? Did she have to get married just to have a man? I had imagined it differently for her some day. She would have had it easier with Pepi. I'm sure I could have talked her out of this marriage, but it's too late now.

Ernilein, I think you are writing less often, but I can understand that you are busier now.

My bridge ladies all send their regards. Bridge is always a great pleasure.

Yesterday I had a nice letter from Mrs. Lazarus [a friend] from Kansas City, a package from Kurt after a long time, and a package from Betty. I was very happy because I needed everything so badly. Paula [former cook] was here and brought me lots of things. She told me she was glad that she could make up a little for all my kindness to her, but she would be happier if she knew I could do things for everybody the way I used to.

Tomorrow is Sigmund's seventy-third birthday. I'm invited for coffee. They can't have more than five or six people because there is not enough space for more in their room!.

Now I'm going to give you a recipe for dumplings made of cottage cheese. It's very, very good because I tried it out:

·500 grams cottage cheese, 50 grams butter, 1 egg, 1 egg yolk and beat the whites, 150 grams bread crumbs, a little lemon peel, and salt and sugar. Cream the butter, put the cheese through a sieve, and then knead it all and add the beaten egg whites. Then make little balls and roll them in the bread crumbs. Cook for ten minutes in salt water. Serve with a little melted butter and bread crumbs. They are also good with sugar and cinnamon.

They asked me at the *Hilfsverein* if it's all right with me that the money that was paid for my passage be returned. I told them it was certainly okay.

Today my adviser was here and said one can get visas via Washington. My dentist told me that the *Hilfsverein* told him the same thing, and he sent a telegram to his daughter in New York. What should one believe? It can drive us to desperation, but what can we do? We have to live through it.

I've been taking English lessons for the past few months. It's very difficult for me, and I wonder if I should continue because I really have no hope of getting out.

Bernhardt is writing desperate letters from Amsterdam, but Kurt seems to be better off. I imagine that he came to an agreement with the bank. Anyway, I'm glad that he'll live more comfortably. He also sends packages to Hanna [Kurt's sister] very often, and I'm sure she can use them.

Herta probably won't get out either, because she certainly wouldn't leave her two children here. They heard about some kind of project in Ecuador, but since they can't take Marianne and Bobby, that probably won't work out.

Now Stevie is home again. I hope he had a good time at camp and that he feels good and will calm down a bit.

I beg you again and again, my dearest, stick together and get along.

Soon it will be the New Year again. One year follows the other, and each year I think, next year I'll be with the children. But, unfortunately, in vain.

Now, my dearest children, I'm closing for today. I greet and kiss all of you.

Lovingly, your Mother

August 30, 1941

My dearest children,

Your letter of August 12 came today, Ernilein, and I was very happy to get it. I can see that all of you are happy and content. How much greater my joy would be if I could take part in everything. Well, maybe I'm still going to see it.

Aunt Paula was just here and showed me the telegram from Alfred, which said that immigration to Cuba is imminent. The *Hilfsverein* will tell us everything else. You can imagine the Ebenstein's happiness.

For me, both Ecuador and Cuba are out of the question. I certainly wouldn't be able to stand Ecuador's climate. And Cuba is so expensive that I don't want to burden you like that. Therefore, I will have to wait until the war is over. One can only pray to stay healthy and live through it. Maybe I'll see you again some day.

I'm curious about who is giving the money for the Ebensteins. Herta was just here and told me that they have started to plan their trip to Ecuador, and she'll tell me when she learns something more.

Ernchen, sit down. I have something to tell you. Linchen's sister is in an old-age home here. She's seventy-three years old and married a seventy-six-year-old man in the home. Isn't that wonderful?

You wrote today that I should send you a copy of the affidavit. I already sent it by registered mail. I paid more than six marks for stamps and can't understand why you haven't received it.

You want to know how many people are in the apartment here? Seven, my dear, and Paula has just as many. In one word, it's just great!

Now, Ruthelchen, you are living with Erna again, and I hope you are both happy about it. I hope, Ruthelein, that you will have your own home again soon. It would be the best thing and, God willing, your wish will be fulfilled.

This morning Clare brought me some mushrooms. I ground them and made "beefsteak" out of them. It tasted wonderful. It is made the same as with beef.

Now, my loved ones, I have to go. I kiss and greet you

Your loving, faithful Mother

September 9, 1941

My dearest Ernilein,

Now is the third time that you celebrate your birthday without me and I don't think that I'll ever be able to wish you a Happy Birthday personally again. But at least I can still do it this way. I wish all of the young people in our friendship circle could be with you. Our New Year will not be very nice, but what good is it to complain? You can't change anything and only pray to God that He will protect us from anything worse.

Now, my dearest child, my beloved child, I want to wish you all the best for your birthday. I hope that your life will be as good as I wish it for you. Then you will never miss anything and you will always be happy and content. How much I would like to give you a present that would give you pleasure. But alas, alas!

Tomorrow I'm invited to Herta's for a birthday coffee and on Sunday I was there to hear Mrs. Bernstein's pupils sing. I was so happy to hear singing once again. And there were beautiful voices among them. [She herself had a beautiful voice.]

Marianne has a lovely voice, reaching very rare heights, and sings very purely. The only thing she's lacking is Reni's temperament. She sang an aria from *Madama Butterfly* very, very beautifully. I was so happy about Reni's letter and the pictures. They both look very good. I'm especially glad about the way she writes about her husband.

Ernilein, if something should happen to me and when the war is over, please get in touch with Erna [a friend with whom she left a lot of her things] at Kantstrasse. She knows about all my affairs. I have talked things over with her and I hope that she will let you know about everything. In the meantime, you probably got in touch with Alfred. He sent two telegrams to his parents, and he wants to have them come to Cuba. Sigmund went to the *Hilfsverein* and from there they cabled to Alfred that he should make arrangements for everything and then there is a possibility that they can leave very quickly. [They never got out, went to Theresienstadt, and presumably were murdered in Auschwitz.]

Love to you all, Mother

September 10, 1941

My dearest Ruthelein,

I hope that you are well and that you still have your job. I can imagine that it's not a very pleasant occupation and I'm praying to God daily to fulfill your wish to have your own home pretty soon so that you'll know where you belong.

Now, my child, I want to wish you all the best for your birthday. This is the eighth time I have to do it this way. From Erna's letter you will see that I gave up hope that I will ever be able to do it in person again. Therefore, take my fervent wishes, my child, and if you will have everything I wish for you, then I know that you'll be taken care of for life and that you'll never have any worries. Ruthelein, how I would love to give you some joy, but unfortunately I can't do anything. But you know that I would love to do it. Reni wrote me a very nice letter and sent me some pictures that made me very happy.

How did Stevie enjoy the summer? Did he quiet down a little bit? I feel very sorry for him. When I think what a wonderful youth you had and now I see how he grows up, it's very sad. But many young people here would like to trade places with him.

Ruthelchen, in one word, it's absolutely hopeless here. I haven't seen Claire [Ruth's mother-in-law] for more than a week. I'm not getting away too much right now because I have so much to do. I really don't know how long I will be able stand it. I'm certainly not going to have a breakdown because of all this work. If I could only sleep better. I've tried to take a sleeping pill, but then I can't get myself together at all the following day.

Tomorrow, I think I'll go and visit Claire after all. I can't be with her too long, anyway, because then I'm all worn out from all her talking. Nobody really looks out for her except for me. Trude [Claire's niece] doesn't need her anymore, so she doesn't even bother with her at all. Those are really not very nice people. Trude is housekeeper in the home of an old Justice. They wont be able to get out anymore, either, because the person who gave them an affidavit died in the meantime.

Now, my dear, I want to close for today. For your new year I again wish you all the best with all my heart.

Warmest regards and kisses for you and for Steve.

Your loving mother.

September 19, 1941

I just came back from Herta's. I thought she had a birthday and, to my surprise, I heard that it was Marianne's birthday. Everybody was together there again, and it was very nice. Reni's letter came on time, to the great joy of Marianne. Suse Cohn [a friend of Marianne] was there, too. I'm supposed to send you best regards. She looks awful. I would never have recognized her. She would like to go to her mother in Brazil, but as long as the war lasts, she probably won't be able to get away. Everybody is crying. Everybody looks sad and worried. The pain that we carry is etched into our faces. Every day brings us new sorrow and grief.

Now, my child, for the New Year, I again wish you all the best. Have a wonderful day and I greet you and embrace you. Please give my regards to Martin, Reni, and Egon. I'm going to answer Reni's letter very soon.

Your loving Mother.

September 20, 1941 [incomplete]

My dearest children,

Today I got your letter of August 31st and was very glad to hear that you're all well.

Ernilein, you write that you are so worn out and nervous. Can't you give up this strenuous work [repairing nylons] and look for something else? You can't ruin your eyes altogether. You write that if there's anything I need, I should write to you. I don't need anything, my child.

What I am really missing is a cup of coffee now and then, especially on days like these when I haven't slept for many hours, and then I have to go back to my work. If you could help me with a little coffee, I would be very grateful. [We did send coffee as often as possible, always hoping it would arrive.] It's very difficult for me to cook here. But in a way it's good to have work, because work helps me over many, many problems.

Yesterday, Hina [the family seamstress] was here and sends her best regards. She sends you all the best for your birthday and the New Year as well. She doesn't think she can visit me very often much longer. I'm sure that all the visiting is going to stop very soon.

Ruthelein, I'm very happy that you like your job. [She worked at a soda fountain in a drug store]. I hope you can keep it for very long. I'm so happy that Stevie had such a good summer. You asked me to include a letter for Reni when I write to Erna, but I can only put two sheets into one envelope! Also, I've written two long letters to Reni in the last few weeks. Didn't she get them?

The Ebensteins are hoping for certain that they can go to Cuba. Alfred seems to have everything ready for them.

September 29, 1941

My dearest Renilein,

Your letter gave me a lot of joy, but what I was really most amused about was what you told me about dirtying all the dishes. [I had told her that during my vacation I dirtied all the dishes on the table because I was so happy that I didn't have to wash them.] That's really just like you. But now I have to cook and do dishes every day, i.e., Mille does the dishes most of the time and I dry them. I wish, my child, that I could do it for you.

The Ebensteins got news from the Cuban ambassador to bring in their papers and get their passports. Alfred has done everything from there and they hope that in two months, the latest, they will be out. Now, Alfred has done it after all and Paula is very proud of her son. I know for sure, Renchen, I would get away from here, too, if Arnold were there. He would have been able to accomplish it. But there's nothing we can do. We just have to live through it.

Renilein, what you write about your father is not quite true. It was not possible for your mother and father to live together. They were mismatched. Your mother had one big fault: she was too economical for your father. If he had only listened to her half the time, he wouldn't have been so badly off financially later. I would like to see how you would feel, my child, if Egon had ten women besides you, on whom he spent all his money. What would you do? But what good is it to talk about all this now? It's all over.

I have to agree with what you write about spoiling you in your upbringing. We loved you, and we let you get away with much too much. But today, Renilein, I'm not sorry that we gave you such a beautiful youth. I wish that Stevie could also have such nice memories. I feel very sorry for him. It's very sad how he gets pushed around. I hope he'll grow up to be a competent, successful human being. I suppose it is better if one is not so well off in one's youth, and one's old age is better, than the other way around. The proof is your grandmother.

Marianne is very unhappy. She has nothing but her work day and night. That she didn't get out is the fault of her parents. But now neither Marianne nor Bobby will be able to leave. [I believe that they were doing forced labor and were, therefore, not permitted to leave.]

The last few days we've had a lot of excitement and upset again, but we also have to get over the fact that *none of my friends can come here to visit anymore*!

I would be very happy, my child, if Egon could get a promotion and earn more money. Maybe your life could then be a little easier.

I'm so glad, Renilein, that your mother is content and happy. You can't imagine how happy that makes me. It is good to know that there is somebody who will take care of her. I wish that Aunt Ruth could be in the same position. Worrying about my children will not end until I close my eyes forever. It's easy to say, my child, "don't worry about us." But nobody can jump over their own shadow.

Wasn't your apartment renovated when you moved in? You're going to have a big mess if they do it now!

September 30, 1941

I didn't have time to finish yesterday. Now it is 5:30 and pretty soon I'll go to temple. It's Kol Nidre night. [It's a mystery to me where she went to temple because almost all of the synagogues were destroyed on Kristallnacht.]

Now, my dearest Renilein, farewell. Give my regards to all our loved ones. I kiss you and embrace all of you and am, as always,

your loving Grandmother

October 1941 [incomplete]

[To Ruth and Erna]

I haven't seen Herta for quite a while, but I'm sure she will visit me on the 9th [Erna's birthday]. She always comes on the days of the birthdays.

Yes, Ernilein, now it's your birthday again, the third one without me. I wonder if you can imagine what days such as this mean for me—the holidays, the birthdays, and the memorial days. To be so alone is terrible! I wasn't too much aware of the most recent holidays because I was so busy cooking that I had no time to think!

I'm glad you bought such a nice car. May it bring good luck to Martin. The main thing is that he stays well. Martin's sister has trouble with her heart, too. She wrote to me yesterday that she will come to visit me when she feels better.

I'm very glad to hear that Stevie gives you so much pleasure. I would like to get another photo of him, but please send two so that I can give one to Clare as well.

I can imagine Reni playing the part of a "real Berliner" [a play that was put on by the Immigrants Mutual Aid Society]. Oh, why can't I share my grandchildren's lives? I have such a longing for all of you. What did I do to have such an old age? Vati is certainly better off than I; at least he has a small space for himself.

Now, my dearest ones, farewell. I greet you and kiss you warmly and am, as always,

Your loving Mother

Regards to everyone.

November 5, 1941

[Note: This is probably one of the last letters we received from my grandmother, and it was a very disturbing because it could have gotten my grandmother into serious trouble. Obviously my aunt and my mother must have written to her about some kind of an argument they had over possessions that we took out of Germany illegally—things that should have been turned in to the authorities. Therefore she had worded her reply with invented names and called herself Aunt Ruchel to fool the censors.]

My dearest Ernilein,

I got a letter today from Stevie's mother [Ruth], in which she writes to me that an argument has broken out among the children of Aunt Ruchel. I am sure that Aunt would be mortified if she knew that. She would certainly have wanted it to be different. Also, I would like to tell you that I am not in any kind of shape to answer anything like this. Don't you know what is going on here? Next to the enormous worries we have here, everything else is incidental. Such letters can get me into Rosa's Sanitarium [which means into jail], so, please, I don't want to hear anything about this anymore. I'm asking you to tell the girls that they should keep the peace. There are many worse things, and their mother is just not feeling well right now. Maybe in a very short while you'll get an answer from someone else that will satisfy the girls. . . .

I would also like to tell you that I would not have thought that of the girls, that they would fight about things like that.

[I don't know what this disagreement between Mother and Aunt Ruth was about, but it upset me badly that they bothered my grandmother with it.]

I can't tell you anything about my leaving here this way or that. As soon as I know anything, I will send you a telegram. [I assume that this pertained to her being shipped out of Berlin.]

Toni and many others can't come to visit me anymore either. You cannot imagine the problems we have here. Aunt Paula and Uncle Sigmund are waiting for an answer whether or not they can leave. Alfred wrote to me this week, as well. But at the moment I cannot answer.

Tomorrow I'm moving into a smaller room again, together with another woman; that is my life now. Renilein, your letter made me very happy. I will answer you soon. Give my regards to everyone, and I embrace all of you.

Your loving Mother

December 3, 1941

My dearest children,

Another week has passed without any news from you and that makes me even sadder. But I have all the patience that I need. One has learned to be very patient.

I had a card from Bernhardt yesterday in which he wrote that they don't know how long they can stay there. I'm very sorry for them. Aunt Hulda [Betty's mother] is now going to be seventy-two years old, and it's too sad. But I'm most sorry for the children.

Maybe you'll write to Arnold that he should write to his mother again soon. I don't think she'll be around much longer. She's getting an injection every day now but keeps losing weight all the time. One can only wish that she won't suffer too long. Everybody whose life is over is to be envied. There's so much dying here.

Clare does not talk to anybody about her situation. If something happens to her, nobody knows anything.

Ruthelchen, did you take an apartment as you wanted, or are you still living with Erna? Do you have a lot of work? I visit Herta more often now. Today, Marianne was home, too. She had an industrial accident, breaking her collarbone, and is in great pain. Herta has the flu, and a wooden beam fell on Willi's foot and broke a bone. You can see that they have enough problems, too, and everything is resting on poor old Mrs. Hyman [Herta's mother]. She runs around like a weasel at the age of seventy-six. Herta is sorry that she didn't place her mother in an old-age home, and she's still going to try it now. I'm afraid she won't succeed.

The news is very, very scarce. One has to wait even if it's very difficult. If only I could have some news from you again, I would be a little calmer. It's surprising that our nerves are still holding out, because so much assails us.

I wrote to Reni directly a few days ago. I don't have any more to tell you today.

I love all of you very much, and I embrace you and kiss you.

Your Mother

[This is the last letter I have from my grandmother. I don't know whether the mail service stopped or there were more letters, which I didn't find in my mother's or my aunt's papers.]

[Postcard written by my grandmother from Berlin to my father in Amsterdam before she was deported to Theresienstadt, the following March 18, 1943]. He answered it on October 27, 1943, according to a notation he made on the postcard.]

Berlin—Fall 1942

Dear Mr. Schlesinger,

Many thanks for your nice letter. I would have written to you sooner, but I am quite depressed and tired, so that I cannot even bring myself to write.

I have no news about your sister Hanna's well-being because Clara can no longer visit me, nor can Arnold's mother or my niece, Ella. You can imagine how lonely I am because of this situation. I am glad that I have my work, but I don't know how long my physical strength will hold out.

I did hear from the children this week. They are all right except for their worry about me. *Twenty-five words cannot really tell much*!

Martha Kaiser [our former chauffeur's daughter] was just here. She sends her regards. I hadn't heard from them for three years. Mrs. Kaiser died.

Please write again soon. With best regards.

Yours,

Jenny Pelz

Edith and Erich said goodbye to me, too.

[My father's cousins, deported to Theresienstadt, where Erich died along with Edith's mother. She was subsequently transported to Auschwitz and survived. After the war, she came to the United States, where she died a few years ago in her nineties, with her sense of humor and love of life intact despite her harrowing experiences.]

[Here is a postcard written to Antonia Schultze from Theresienstadt, dated October 3, 1943.]

My dearest Anton,

I only want to tell you that I'm quite well and I hope the same for you. I only wish that you can acknowledge this card as soon as possible. Letters and packages get here very well because the mail is working perfectly. Many of my acquaintances are getting mail every day, and I'm always jealous. If I could have forms from the Red Cross, I could also write to the children.

Tomorrow is Ruth's birthday and on Saturday it's Erna's. You can imagine how I feel when I think of the children. Please give my regards to Erna Freitag [a friend] and tell her she should also remember me. More than ever, I'm asking all of you not to forget me. Please don't make me wait for an answer for too long. I'm waiting for it longingly.

To you, dear Anton, I'm sending my warmest regards.

Yours,
Jenny

*Anton(ia) was a former employee who helped Jenny until the last day. After the war, she added Jenny's name to that of her late husband on his gravestone at the Jewish cemetery, with the words "Murdered in Auschwitz."

Amsterdam
August 30, 1945

My dearest Erna,

I received your letter of August 17 yesterday, and I was so happy to hear from you. It was the first communication from you in years. I will try to answer your letter as best I can.

It certainly is an accident that we lived through all this. It is because we were *Mischlinge* [of mixed heritage]. My mother was an Aryan, so we had only two Jewish grandparents. Therefore we were not sent to Poland, but we stayed in Theresienstadt.

I had a very close acquaintance in Theresienstadt who had a very good position, at least at the time when your poor mother was deported. When I went to him crying and seeking help for your mother, he tried—for my sake—to do everything to keep her out of the transport to Poland. He gave her name as being family. Your mother was aware of this, too, because she also knew him, and she was very happy about his trying to help.

For some days I was really hopeful, but at the last minute his request was refused, and she had to leave with the last transport in May [1944].

I was with her until the last moment. It was almost worse for me than for her. It was as if they took my own mother away. . . . I am positive she did not know what was going to happen to her in Poland. That's my only consolation. Your consolation should be—and must be—that she certainly did not suffer because, upon their arrival in Auschwitz, the older people were immediately put into so-called showers. But according to eyewitness accounts, instead of water, gas was released, and people fell asleep forever. It was, I suppose, a "humane" death compared to reports of eyewitnesses who watched people slowly starve to death.

Dr. Lissauer's [Jenny Frohmann's employer] sister, and her son Walter, died in Bergen-Belsen from hunger and typhus, and I had the personal account of a very good acquaintance who buried both of them.

When you hear these horrible accounts, one has to be grateful that your dear ones did not have to go through this. Your dear mother was terribly sad that she had to leave, but was really quite calm when I told her, certainly against my better knowledge and with a bleeding heart, that everything would be all right. And she promised to be brave and to hold out that one day she could see you again.

Well, enough of this horror. Unfortunately, we can't change any of the past.

My acquaintance was sent away in November after all, despite all his connections. And he also died with most of the others.

Yesterday, Lisa had a baby, a very strong boy, over six pounds.

I cannot believe that Betty [Lisa's mother] is obviously not coming back, either. She always knew how to work things out, and she certainly was not spoiled, and could do all kinds of work. Maybe she will return, but I honestly don't believe it.

I expected that Bernhardt [Betty's husband] wouldn't come back. He was already half crazy when they shipped him out, and only did stupid things [like coming out of hiding, taking his wife with him. Their daughters stayed in hiding in Amsterdam and survived.] The Aufrechts were together with your mother in Theresienstadt, and she also told me he did a lot of foolish things. For example, he stole bread from his comrades, and was punished for that.

[The second page of this letter is missing, but I'm continuing on page 3.]

All the stores here are still all in trouble, and everything is really very uncertain. The Oxyde Company, my former employer, is still in operation. I go there every day for a few hours, and Elsa [her sister] as well, to see what is new. Right now, we're getting a little money just to get by. . . .

I often tell my friends, "Maybe the best thing would have been if they had gassed us, too." I'm sure many people here would have welcomed it. All of us at Theresienstadt almost met the same fate as those in Auschwitz. We can be grateful for the resistance of the Commandant, that the gas chambers did not work due to some mistake in the structure of the building. If the Russians had come four weeks later for the liberation, they would probably not have found anybody alive. You see, everything is fate.

I'm enclosing a letter your dear mother gave me for you, listing everything she left in Berlin with various people. As soon as I can correspond with Germany, I will give you news immediately. I hope you will get at least a good part of your things back. But one also has to figure on the possibility that everything was destroyed by bombs.

Give my regards to Reni and to your husband. I embrace you warmly.

Yours,
Jenny (Frohmann)

This is the letter given to Jenny Frohmann in Theresienstadt.

Dear Jennylein,

Because I know your faithful friendship and dependability, I'm writing this for the children. Erna's address is 5 Parkvale, Brookline, Massachusetts.

At Erna Freitag's house, Kantstrasse 76, there is a suitcase with linens, my fur piece, dresses, suits, hats, and pocketbooks—all I had. Also the beautiful bag that Aunt Paula gave me as her last present; there are 3 meters of very valuable lace, a watch, costume jewelry and other things; also the beautiful embroidered pillow. I'm sure that Erna will return everything.

At Antonia Schulze's, Trelleborgerstrasse 61, there are my

suitcases, my knitted afghan, shoes, 2 fur pieces that I want Reni to have in case the children get all these things, as a present for the birth of her child. My beautiful embroidered bag, the last thing I made; and one large black leather bag; my wedding ring; my black enamel brooch, as well as some costume jewelry, and embroidered white tablecloths. I am sure that Miss Schulze will also return the things that I have not listed here, because she always liked the children so very much.

At Mrs. Hinze's house, Herderstrasse 13, is my fur lining, fur pieces and several other things. I know that she will also return everything.

The superintendent's wife at Bayrischer Platz 5 took everything out of my room and told Mrs. Berlowitz that when I come back she will return everything. There was one 3-meter long rug runner, a very beautiful sewing table, a couch with pillows, 2 chairs with cane and pillows, a floor lamp with indirect light, a large mirror with a wide silver frame, a brand new suitcase, a packed knapsack, 5 pairs of shoes, brown, blue, grey, black; all my dresses, coats, slips, underwear. One white armoire, one white dresser, one cupboard with dishes. Everything was bought for America, and was of the best quality.

Unfortunately I did not find Sigmund and Paula here anymore. They were deported before I arrived. Clare died on March 4, 1943. Mille and Adolf Aufrecht died too: he, on September 19, 1943 and Mille on March 1, 1944. Willi also died on March 5, 1943.

August 21, 1945 [written after we received positive information that my grandmother had perished]

My dearest Erna,

I received your meaningful letter about an hour ago and we know now that we don't have our mother anymore. I so much wanted to see Mutti just once more. I clung to a small ray of hope that somebody had hidden her, but now it's all over. Mutti would be so happy that after all the hard years I am happy again and especially that you are content and happy. [Ruth had also remarried.]

Erna, dear, I can't believe that nine years ago in Haifa I said good-bye to Mutti and that it was really the last time she embraced me. I am so unhappy. Little Erna, I promise you—and I know it would be according to Mutti's wishes, for it was her fervent wish until the end of her days—whatever happens let us stick loyally together, let us not quarrel or argue about trifles, because compared to what has happened to both of us, what is going on now is nothing but trifles. I can imagine how upset Reni is. She was so attached to Mutti. Arnold will also be upset, because he too loved her and now he also knows that his mother is dead.

I can hardly think! I should really come home immediately, but I can't leave Freddy [Ruth's second husband] here all alone. He would be so lonely without me, and there has been a lot of work here for the past two weeks. Otherwise, I would certainly have joined you, if only to have a good cry together with you. So long, Ernalein, my big sister, now there are only the two of us and our two kids.

Warmly and with love,

Yours, Ruth

Best regards to Martin, too.

Ernalein, I want to tell you something else which you should understand and don't be offended. Get along with Martin. He is good to you, and he wants the best for you. Be quiet, even if you know that he is wrong. That will make life so much easier. Let us try to become as much like Mutti as possible. Then, all the love and kindness she always surrounded us with will bear fruit. Please don't be mad about what I'm saying; you know I love you.

Your "little" sister,

Ruth

Dear Erna,

As you can imagine, our dear Ruth was very upset. I certainly wouldn't mind letting her come home (which was her first thought), but now she has decided otherwise and wants to stay with me for the last week. I am doing my best to calm her down.

What can one say about all these inhuman atrocities! The only thing I did when I got the message last year of my mother's death in Theresienstadt was to say to myself, "You mustn't think about it if you don't want to go out of your mind!" Unfortunately, one can't even count on the swine being punished, however inadequately, for their crimes. (Oh, "Nobody knew anything, and nobody is responsible!")

I hope to see you next week in good health. My best regards to everybody,

Fred

[This is a letter from our friend, Jenny Frohmann, in Amsterdam, who wrote to me on February 15, 1946, after the sudden death of my father in a traffic accident in the Netherlands.]

My dearest Reni,

As I write to you today, I wish it were another occasion, but I'm sending you my condolences on the death of your father. The letter from Christine [my father's second wife] was sent to you yesterday. I'm sure you got it in the meantime. So you know the cause of his death.

To give you words of comfort is very difficult for me because I know from my own experience that big and long separations seem to make the pain much less than if you had lived closely with him all these years. I hope with all my heart that you're not going to suffer too much from this news.

I hadn't seen your father for a very long time. Shortly after our return from camp, I certainly saw him and didn't think he looked very well, even if he said that he was feeling all right. Later, he was always traveling when I tried to see him. Inasmuch as we were in different parts of the city, I couldn't see him whenever he was in Amsterdam.

Christl suffered much more from his death than I would ever have thought possible. I'm awfully sorry for her but one can't help her at all.

The last wish of your father was that he be cremated, and this was done. At the moment, however, she doesn't know where she will get the money to pay for this. The financial circumstances are pretty unclear, but it seems to me that there is no money, or very little, available. The furniture represents most of the value. But you, as his daughter, have the right to inherit all that, according to the laws here.

I certainly expect that you will let Christl represent you and your interests here at the court, and that you also will leave the furniture for her use because she's depending on using it to rent the apartment, so that she can have the barest necessities for her living expenses. She can only get all these things, as far as I know, if she gets your agreement. Therefore, I am asking you to sign the power of attorney that Christl sent to you and send it back immediately. And I don't have to tell you that, in my opinion, you can trust her completely. She would rather starve to death than take anything that does not belong to her. As I told you, at the moment she seems to be standing in front of nothing.

And now to something more pleasant. Your Sylvia [my older daughter] seems to be awfully cute. Your mother writes to me regularly about you and your child, and I only regret that I can't be with you as I was before. Maybe you'll have a photo of your whole family so that at least I can share things with you through pictures. Here among the few things that I found, I also found some photos from your earliest childhood, and I think that Sylvia looks like you. I also found a childhood picture of Steven. He was such a beautiful child, and I would be interested to know how he looks today. Inasmuch as your Aunt Ruth never wrote to me, I cannot ask her. But maybe you will have an opportunity to send me a photo of Stevie.

When you have time and you feel like it, I would be happy to hear about your life there, about your husband and what he's doing. So write me something more about your life. In spite of the late and long deprivations, my interests have remained the same, and I will never forget that you were my everything when you were a baby. I carried you around in my arms for days and weeks because you were so spoiled. In the meantime, you're a young woman and mother, and thus I can see how old I am.

Now, my little Reni, don't be too sad; take everything the way it is. I'm also going to write to Mutti in a few days. Give her my regards in the meantime. I embrace you and greet you. And give your Sylvia a kiss for me. I would like to spoil her as much as I spoiled you. And to your husband, even if I don't know him, my best regards.

Your old Aunt Jenny [Frohmann]

Berlin-Pankow, August 1, 1946
Trelleborgerstrasse 61

Dearest Erna,

I received your kind, detailed letter of June 15 two days ago (your dear mother's birthday), which I appreciate very much. I have waited a long time for some sign of life from you or Ruth. I couldn't write because, due to the war, I lost all my address books. So I had to wait patiently until I heard from you. Recently, a friend of Reni came to me and, at the request of your daughter, informed me of your mother's death. She herself got the news several weeks ago, but she apparently didn't find the time to reach me personally. I must tell you that the death of your dear mother upset me deeply.

Last summer, when there was an appeal on the radio asking anyone who had relatives or acquaintances in Theresienstadt to report to the Jewish community office, I went immediately to the Iranische Strasse to inform them that I wanted to take your mother in. But, unfortunately, her name was not on the list. I was very unhappy. The man there, noticing my sadness, tried to console me by telling me that she might have escaped to Switzerland. A number of elderly people had been taken there by the Red Cross, he added; maybe Mrs. Pelz was among them. But all my inquiries were in vain. Then from time to time I went to the Oranienburger Strasse [location of the community center at the time], but the answer was always negative. I feared the moment when you and Ruth would ask me about your mother's whereabouts.

I'm not sure if you know that I was very close to her until the end. Through the years I took care of her and surrounded her with the love she missed and deserved for all the love and kindness she gave to other people. I brought her any food, wine, etc. that I could get hold of. You know the Jews received hardly any vegetables and no fruit at all. I brought her everything she missed. For her birthday and for Christmas I surrounded her with special love. I wanted to make her feel the magic of home, and I managed to make her feel happy for as long as I was with her. In the end, she ran out of warm panties, gloves, stockings, etc., so I supplied her with those things, too. I was able to do it, because I had customers who supplied me with various things.

I think you know that the good lady went to work in a factory despite her age, because she hoped she could remain in Berlin by doing so. She did expect the terrible deportation, and she was aware of it. She kept a knapsack packed with bare essentials in her apartment, but it remained there, because she was taken from her workplace and deported to the hopelessness of foreign lands. I was desperate when I learned about it. I was absolutely unable to do anything. Those who didn't live here at that time do not know how deep human suffering can be. So much cruelty is inconceivable. One went from one fear to another.

In the end, when I sat in your mother's apartment, I was so full of fear that, just like your mother, I trembled with each ringing of the doorbell for fear the Gestapo were at the door. How often I went down the backstairs out into the street. The last few times I always took my maid along, because I was afraid that they would catch me.

In 1940, I was reported to the Gestapo for anti-fascist behavior and friendliness toward Jews, and was pulled out of bed at seven o'clock in the morning. I was held in custody the whole day. After endless interrogations they let me go at eight o'clock in the evening. After that nothing happened, but fear never left me.

Nevertheless, I helped my friends wherever I could. For me it was a simple human duty to interfere helpfully whenever the law and the authorities failed completely. I considered Hitler's government a regime of terror from the first day. I rose against it in both word and deed. My Emma [maid] often feared that they would arrest me when I came home late at night. Well, everything worked out for me, but not for your dear mother. Believe me, Erna, I mourn deeply with you and Ruth. Rest assured of my sympathy and please express my feelings to Ruth too.

I have kept my apartment, even though it and the furniture suffered substantial damage due to the war. I have put everything back in order and am happy to have a roof over my head. I hope it will remain so, because I have already had to have occupation troops in my apartment for five weeks. My store was totally destroyed by bombs, and now, a year later, I am ready to build it up again. I lost most of my warehouse storage, because it was kept in bank safes, but now these safes are inaccessible.

But it doesn't matter. I'm happy that the horrible war is over and that we can again sleep at night. It is impossible to describe the deadly fear. We often lay trembling on the floor of the shelters when the bombs struck. The earth and the walls would shake so. During the last year, I would leave my home every morning at eight o'clock and move into the bunker, coming home only during the morning hours. When I was barely home, the sirens would start to shriek again. You can believe me that those years devastated our nerves. Because of enormous exertion and the hardships, I have developed a serious weakness of the heart muscle. And how am I to have it attended to now?

My sister and her children were able to keep their apartments, and that is really great luck. Unfortunately, my sister's oldest son was killed in Russia in the bitterly cold winter. He suffered terribly. Her youngest son is still a prisoner of war in Russia, and we haven't had any news from him for over a year. We hope he'll come back soon. My sister's children are all married except for Erna, who was the eldest. She is a kind soul, but unfortunately is also paralyzed. She is, however, in her touching care for everybody, a blessing for the whole family. My brother-in-law's relatives who lived in Pomerania were forced to leave their homes.

The plight of the refugees is horrible. What I have witnessed is indescribable. And all this because of a handful of criminals. I cannot get it through my head that the Germans could ever have agreed to carry out such monstrous orders. I heard plenty and took care to spread the information in my own circle of friends, but not everybody believed it. People often said, "No, I can't believe it, this can't be true." I relied on what I had experienced, on what I had heard in the American and British broadcasts. But I never could have imagined the extent of the crimes. I had already deeply condemned what I had experienced through my Jewish friends. That was the greatest cruelty and infamy. On July 20, 1944, I was in Dresden, where I had been evacuated for one year. There was a son there, a *Mischling*, the nephew of my American woman friend. We both could only say, "What a shame that it [the attempted assassination of Hitler] failed."

I still don't have any news from my friend. She lived for two years in Havana, Cuba, and then got a visa to go to America. I learned that she left for New York. I really worry about her. She had two brothers in Dresden, both married. I took care of them for many years. Since 1936, I have supported both families with 50 marks a month each, in addition to clothing, underwear, and food. I considered it my duty, because the hands of my friends in America were tied. I suppose she worried a lot as she had a tendency to depression. She also had close relatives in Prague. I even went to see them once more during the war (someone got a visa for me). At that time, they were still living in their home. What might have become of them? They were so kind and warm-hearted. I could do nothing for them, either. The Jews of Prague were all deported, as far as we had heard. Who can bear so much grief?

Now I want to ask a big favor of you which I'm sure you will fulfill. My friend's address was: Mrs. Rosa Kühnrich, Havana, Cuba, D'Estrampes 163. Her landlord and his wife were very nice people, but I don't know their name. She had a nice little apartment. The letters always arrived when mailed to the above address. Would you be good enough to write to the landlord and ask for her whereabouts? She certainly left her forwarding address. Maybe this way I could learn what has become of her. You might mention in your letter that she shared the apartment with Mrs. Blanka Muhlbauer and Mrs. Fröhlich (both from Vienna). They arrived in Havana a little later the same year, 1939. Maybe somebody knows the address of these ladies. Supposedly, they also went to New York. Do you know anyone in New York who could check the phone book? It's possible they changed their names or got married again.

I want to try everything in order to find out what happened to my friend. I love her very much. For me she was the embodiment of everything noble, and I hope with all my heart that she is still alive. I cannot find any explanation why she still hasn't written. It could be that Blanka Muhlbauer, who is also a kind person and who stayed in my home for a few nights before leaving for Cuba with Mrs. Fröhlich, lost my address. My house number was 33A before, and I already notified the post office accordingly. Look what's buzzing around in my head, but I am sure you can understand me. So, please, do me the favor I ask of you. And include a return envelope.

I already know from your mother that you, my dear Erna, have remarried. She showed me pictures of you and your husband and of Reni and her husband as well. I was with her often. Whenever I could bring sunshine into her room and a small piece of blue sky, I did so. I also heard about Ruth's fate, and I am very glad that she got married again. She is also a dear person and deserves to be happy. I would be so glad to receive pictures from all of you. I will also send you my picture. But I have to borrow a camera, because I have lost mine someplace. I have also lost all my dowry linen—everything, everything. I have two big suitcases in the Sudetenland. Most of my linen was still brand new. My new lingerie (which had been custom-made by Grunfeld [a fancy linen store in Berlin] only two years ago) and your mother's suitcase in Zullichau, where I had left them in care of my maid's family, were all destroyed in the fires. I kept my new wool coats and suits at the Deutsche Bank. You know, people used to call that "risk distribution."

Everything I kept in Weissig near Dresden was saved. Among these things was your mother's marten stole and her Gobelin bag containing your father's wedding ring and a small box of jewelry. I don't remember what else there is, but everything is there, it's just not unpacked. Your mother had a big cardboard box in my shop from which, little by little, she took things to use for bartering. There were fabrics, linen, etc. Both my employees, Mrs. Litten and Mrs. Luedecke, know all about it. I still have a large tablecloth and one for a small table (both embroidered) which I received as a gift from your mother, either for my birthday or for Christmas. My employees know all about these, too. I also have the knitted or crocheted travel blanket.

All this is available to you, of course. For you, every piece holds a memory. Your mother's hands touched them. Furthermore, she gave me a bronze statuette of a nude female figure (I would call it "the drinking woman") and a vase, which, amazingly enough, survived intact. The vase is unusual and will certainly please you. I myself have lost almost all my china and glassware. Only a small amount remained, some belonging to your mother. If I only knew how I could get everything to you. I'd like to do it as soon as possible so you can have them soon.

Your mother also gave me a farewell letter [never received] for both of you, which I deposited at the bank for security reasons. Unfortunately, there is no way to get it now. To my knowledge, your mother kept a lot of linen and also her silver fox with Frau Dr. Freitag. But I can't tell you if these things still exist. Your mother told me only that Erna Freitag was wearing the fox. She told me, too, to wear the marten stole, but I refused. That which was entrusted to me I took care of like a treasure. The fur was always well stored. At the moment, it is hanging in the fresh air. Again, I'm glad to have saved these belongings of your mother. For you and Ruth there is a bit of *Heimat* [home] attached to them, isn't there, my dear child?

How are you doing there? Does Ruth live in the same city? Does she have a nice apartment, too? Did the separation from Germany hurt you a great deal emotionally?

If you saw our once-beautiful Berlin today, your heart would break. Rubble and ruins. Pankow fared best of all. From my window I see intact buildings and gardens, but in our hearts all of us are broken. What more awaits us here? Yes, I certainly would be glad to receive a little package from you. Everything would be useful. Because there is nothing to buy here anymore. We really have become poor.

Next week I'll get a card from the UNRRA and send it to you special delivery. I just wanted to get the letter on the way to inform you of everything that has happened here. And now, so long. My best wishes to you and also to Ruth. My regards to your husband as well. I'm glad to know that you are happy, you really deserve it. You always were an honest, dear, and good person. I embrace you in old faithfulness.

Yours,

Antonia [called "Anton"]

Berlin-Pankow, August 23, 1946
61 Trelleborgerstrasse II

Dearest Erna,

Today I am aware that my first letter has not yet reached you.

It is touching that you should want to send me a package and I really don't know how to repay you. I don't know your financial situation well enough to feel comfortable with accepting it. Since you, like all other emigrants, left the country with nothing, you must be working very hard to earn enough money to live on. Therefore, it bothers me to impose expenses and inconvenience on you. My friend Rosel Kühnrich was my big hope, since she is a wealthy woman. She owned stocks in Bethlehem Steel, so you can very well imagine that she is able to send packages to all her friends and relatives. More so, as she knows that I never abandoned her siblings during all those terrible years.

Yesterday I read in the paper that a Berlin woman complained that she still hadn't received mail and packages from her relatives in America though she knows that they had been sent to her. She learned about it from relatives in Hamburg. That could also be the case with Rosel, I suppose. During the heavy air raids I was evacuated to a place near Dresden, where I lived one year with Rosel's relatives. Rosel had a sister who was married to a Christian and lived in Weissig near Dresden. This young woman died when her son, Günther, was two years old. The brother-in-law remarried, this time to a Christian. The couple had a girl, who is now twenty-two years old. Günther is twenty-five. Günther and I have developed a beautiful friendship. We understand each other very well. I'm not too fond of the girl, Ursel, or her mother, because of their political views.

Her father joined the party in 1933 and attained the rank of chairman. For that, he was put in jail for one year as a political prisoner. The family was absolutely crazy about Hitler. Günther and I could say and prove whatever we wanted, but they wouldn't believe us, and we often had unpleasant arguments. It was, from a psychological point of view, a puzzle for me how someone who had first been married to a Jewish woman could identify with such a false doctrine. I could write whole volumes about my experiences with people in those horror years. My friend Rosel was deeply attached to Günther, and I'm sure she'll be happy to know that he and I are such close friends.

The boy was emotionally deprived during those long years. His stepmother was quite kind to him, but she didn't understand his emotional needs.

I hope with all my heart that you succeed in the search for my friend Rosel or one of her friends. If only I knew Blanka's maiden name. She had a brother who was a bank director in Vienna and who had left the country immediately in 1933 for America. His first name was Emil, and he went to New York. He always called me Toni and I called him Emil, and so I forget his last name and all my notes are still at the bank. Emil is also somewhat obligated to me, so I'm sure he would be eager to tell me everything he knows about Rosel. Maybe it is possible to find something out by way of Havana or by checking the New York telephone book.

I also heard that Blanka Muhlbauer started her own business as a corsetiere and that Mrs. Fröhlich is supposed to be working on her own as a dressmaker. Could one get some information through the Jewish community? My dear Erna, I'm sorry to ask so much of you, but you cannot imagine how much I miss Rosel! And how important it is for me to find out what has become of her! I know that she'll help me. We had agreed that after the end of the war I would come to New York, even if only for a while.

For the time being, there is probably no way to do it, but one day it will be possible, and then we'll see each other again, too. I look forward to seeing you and Ruth, because both of you are my dear friends from my youth. How many unforgettable hours we spent together! I still see you as a young woman in your lovely house in Zehlendorf, holding your baby in your arms. I remember you had a "flame"—I have forgotten his name—when you were a very young girl and that Ruth had one as well. His name was "Egon."

Whatever became of Magda Heimann? You used to have two nice girlfriends, and one of them had a sister who died, as I remember. And all the beautiful parties at the Pelzes'. When one thinks back today, it's as if it were the land of milk and honey. When I come to visit you someday, we'll talk all about it.

I have already heard from your mother about Ruth's marital troubles. What has become of Arnold? Does Ruth have a nice husband again? I also cannot imagine that Betty Grünberg is no longer alive. That kind, warm-hearted human being! Is there no news about Aunt Hulda, either?

It was lucky that you two girls left the country just at the right time. Therefore you had at least a few quiet years, as far as your worries about your mother permitted. Fortunately, you haven't been through the nightly bomb attacks. We have missed five years worth of sleep here. Even now I can't get used to it. I often can't fall asleep at night. The deadly fear is still in my bones.

I hope that one day I'll be able to repay your kindness and love. I have always said that every ray of sun that one gives out will come back a thousand times over. That's what I've clung to all these years, and in so doing have remained true to myself. It makes me happy to receive a package from you.

I have almost no underwear. My clothes are so threadbare and patched up that I'm ashamed. I kept the worst pieces while some of the new lingerie was partly destroyed in the fires, and the rest is still in the bank. The same goes for the shoes.

I hope to reopen the shop in the fall. But the rebuilding is fraught with so many difficulties. There are no building supplies available anywhere. The glass panes are the worst problem. In my bedroom, for example, there are whole window panes missing, all lost in the insane struggle for Berlin. Soap is also a big problem here. During the war we could do very little laundry. For the body we used claysoap, which was totally useless.

Last week I had to undergo jaw surgery. It was very strenuous for me. I'm now in need of care. We Germans no longer have any reserves of strength.

So, my dear Erna, stay well and give my regards to your husband, although we still haven't met. Say hello to Reni and Ruth, too.

Always yours,
Toni

Berlin-Pankow 11/26/46
61 Trelleborgerstrasse II

My dear Ruth,

My darling little Ruth, to me you will always be "little Ruth," God bless you. I was so happy when I received your letter on 11/18, eight days ago. In the same mail I got a letter from my dear Erna dated November 1. I waited eagerly for your letters. I knew that you'd write.

Yes, my little Ruth, you were my favorite among your siblings. I myself was only a child when I came to your mother, and she always treated me as one of you. Ruth, as a small child you were so sweet. How sweet and charming your little mouth chatted! My dear mother couldn't wait for me to come home at night to give her a report on you. If I didn't begin at once, she asked what did little Ruth say today? You always had something kind and nice to tell. At that time, and even later, every day was full. We lived lovingly with and for each other.

What was the name of your first flame, wasn't it Egon? When your dear mother took me to a dance, you both brought a lot of things to make me beautiful. And in the evenings, when we got ready for bed, each of you had to plait one of my braids. Ruth, one could howl like a lapdog recalling how much we had and how much we had to give up. Your mother and I always talked about you. Ruth, every time I visited your mother she embraced and kissed me. The poor soul missed both of you so much! And she always hoped to see you again. It is sad to talk about all this.

I'm attaching a postcard from Theresienstadt which I recently found. At least it is written in her own hand and therefore a treasure,

Postcard sent by Jenny from Theresienstadt

isn't it? I heard from your dear mother that your marriage didn't turn out as you hoped. It is a pity about Arnold. He was a dear man. Yes, dear Ruth, you and your fellow Jews had to travel many roads with thorns and sharp stones. I always admired you and Erna for how bravely you both went to foreign countries and how you coped with life, although it was often so hard.

I'm happy to know that you found happiness with your new husband. I'm very pleased for you. I hope that the day will come, after all, when I'll be able to visit you. I hope that I will live to see it. You know then we'll chat and cry to our heart's desire. This is part of it—when we exchange lovely memories. As I write these words, tears come to my eyes; but I'm not ashamed of them.

What has become of our beautiful Germany? Wherever the eye can see—only ruins! You can't find your way around in this city anymore! The building at 55 Friedrichstrasse is also destroyed. It was your childhood home, wasn't it? But it wasn't *Heimat*:

Die Heimat ist, wo man Dich gern erscheinen,
ungern wandern sieht.
Sie ist's, wenn auch in weiter Ferne,
die Mutter sang Dein Wiegenlied.

Home is where they're happy
when you arrive and miss you when you leave.
It is, even when far away,
where your mother sang your cradle song.

I fervently hope that you feel at home over there. I hope you have found a circle of congenial, nice people with whom you can feel comfortable.

It's wonderful that you enjoy the medical job so you can be the best companion to your husband. Is your husband also from Germany? Your home looks very nice. This is a nice "topping off" of all the hard years of work. And when your son finally comes home, your happiness will be complete. Where did your Stefan fight, or hasn't he been in the war?

I still hope that one day somebody will come to visit me personally, that somebody will ring the doorbell and bring greetings from beloved people. There are many people overseas whom I value.

Yes, the Nazis made so many people infinitely unhappy, and the German people as well. Hard and terrible years lie behind us. Ruth, believe me, the Nazis acted so cleverly from the start that nobody could say anything. You can see that from the many victims of the concentration camps. People only whispered here, otherwise they risked disappearing forever. I certainly risked a lot, but luckily I talked mostly with like-minded people. Except that one time when somebody in our building reported me to the authorities for anti-fascist views and friendliness toward Jews. I was lucky that it turned out well, otherwise I wouldn't be alive, either. On the other hand, I wouldn't have missed much considering what remained for us.

We now live from day to day. I never heard people talking about food so much as I do now. People are suffering a lot of hardship here. Because of the hard years, the privation, and the strain, I have severe heart muscle weakness. And there is a shortage of medications, tonics, and proper nourishment. Many people are dying of hunger! I bought a garden last fall in which my Emma and I have worked very hard. Therefore, we didn't have to go hungry because we had vegetables, lettuce, and even a little fruit during the summer. But fat, milk, and meat-protein are lacking. Some people, enduring great hardships, are going out of town for vegetables and potatoes. You see haggard, pale faces of people almost breaking down under unbearable burdens. I wouldn't have the strength to do this.

So you can't even imagine how much I look forward to the package. I wrote to Mrs. Hinze today telling her that she can expect a pleasant surprise. As soon as I receive the package, I'll send her a telegram to come. I want us both to open the package together, something which will undoubtedly be in accordance with the wishes of two kind-hearted contributors. She should feel the same joy as I. I'm sure we both will gaze wide-eyed at the gifts like a Kate Kruse doll. I would feel better when she is with me as we unpack, so that she doesn't have to fear that she'll be at a disadvantage. After all, she doesn't know me at all.

My shop isn't open yet. I anticipate it will happen at the beginning of the year. I got my license today. The completion of the building is quite difficult as there are no supplies. In March 1943, Goebbels shut down our whole industry to sustain the "total war." We weren't consulted; only appointed people screamed their "yes." What a farce it was!

I think Erna told you that miraculously I was able to keep my apartment. However, it was badly damaged. But it's O.K. now, except for many broken windows. In my bedroom there is not a single windowpane left. Besides, I lost all my dowry linen and all my lingerie, as well as a large part of my stock, which was kept out of town. All banks are closed for us. But I must console myself; other people lost more.

For the last eight days I have had a girlfriend from the Sudetenland staying with me. She had left her home like a beggar, and on the way was robbed of even the very little she had left. The plight of the refugees is terrible. My girlfriend, who lives in Meissen, sleeps on a sofa at night without taking off her clothes because she lacks a blanket. Millions of people in Europe live in such misery. I gave her some of the few pieces of underclothes I still had. If you have some cast-offs, a slip, camisoles, panties, etc., I would be grateful to get them, as well as some black and white thread, a pair of dress shields, a little sewing silk, and some darning-thread in blue and black. We really don't have any whole pairs of stockings at all, and we can't darn them. And if you could send me some milk powder, I would appreciate it very much. I'm sure the time will come when I'll be able to repay you for it.

For all you have done I send you my heartfelt gratitude and thank you for your love.

I greet you and embrace you.

Your old Anton

August 31 1947

Yesterday I read in the paper that beginning September 15, it will be permitted to send up to 2 kg [roughly 4.5 pounds] parcels to the U.S.A. This will make many things easier. Therefore, I will wait until September 15.

I also remembered what your dear mother told me concerning her last will. She said she made a last will just in case she would no longer be able to wear the jewelry she left to you. In that case, the pieces should be divided fairly. She said, "I know that I really don't need a will for my children, because even without it they will share everything fairly." She regretted only that she had followed the order to turn in Vati's ring. She didn't follow my advice to buy a smaller and cheaper one with only one stone and hand it in instead. I hope you have saved most of the beautiful jewelry. Your mother really did own pieces of the highest quality. I remember especially the pearl necklace and the emerald ring. Wear them all in good health in honor of your beloved, deceased mother.

Always,
Your Anton

My grandparents' Silver Wedding Anniversary (second marriage for my grandmother). Her first husband died at age 36. Left to right: My mother, Arnold, Ruth, my grandparents and I. It was the last family celebration before the Nazis took over and Ruth and Arnold left Germany.

Fifty Years After Kristallnacht, November 9, 1938

Why, suddenly, am I a sought-after "celebrity"? I have been interviewed and photographed for the magazine section of *The* [Boston] *Sunday Herald*. I have been taped for a radio program. I have been asked to speak at two synagogues. And all because, unfortunately, I was an eyewitness to one of the most tragic, most unforgettable events in the history of our people.

Kristallnacht—the Night of the Broken Glass—on November 9-10, 1938. I was seventeen years old. Not too many of us are left and not everyone who has gone through the experience is able to talk about it. People want to hear what it was like from someone who was there, what it was like to live through that nightmare.

I remember! Glass breaking through most of the night. Synagogues burning and desecrated—the glow of fires visible in the sky. Jewish males rounded up and collected in local prisons to be sent to concentration camps. Some of the men, including my brother-in-law, had been warned by decent Germans—yes, there were some of those—to try to escape by riding trains all night. However, when he called home during the night, he was told by his wife that the police had been there looking for him, and if he didn't return, they would take her and their young son. Needless to say, he came home. (This story was obviously told to me later. I was not married in 1938 and had no brother-in-law at the time.)

Kristallnacht was the final blow that convinced German Jewry that Hitler meant what he had threatened in his *Mein Kampf* and in countless speeches: He was going to make Europe *judenrein* (free of Jews).

All he had been looking for was a reason to arouse the masses. When the young third secretary at the German embassy in Paris was shot by a distraught Polish Jew, seventeen years old, he had the excuse he was looking for to unleash a "spontaneous people's action." How strange it was that all the paint used to smear the Jewish storefronts with swastikas, Stars of David, and "Jew" seemed to have come out of the same pot all across the city of Berlin. It was clearly not a "people's action" but one carefully planned and prepared by the government.

The next morning we surveyed the damage. We were appalled and frightened. Broken glass covered the sidewalks, storefronts were marked up, windows smashed, and extensive looting had taken place. People were being beaten in the streets. Our Temple was burning and the Torah scrolls had been carried outside onto the streets and trampled on.

I remember a young man in uniform standing there, gleefully watching the acts of destruction, when a middle-aged woman said to him: "I was a nurse in the last war, and I treated Jews and Christians alike!" He glared at her and said menacingly: "Did you ever see a concentration camp?" She left very quickly.

Now I am asked to recall those terrible days. The memory has been buried all these years. I can hardly believe it has been fifty years—a lifetime. I can speak about it now with some detachment. It is as if I am recounting history, not events that I have personally experienced. Did I really live through six years of Nazi rule?

I often feel guilty. I am here to tell the story while so many members of my family and my people perished. But I cannot be silent. I speak to schoolchildren about my experience, to warn them of the dangers of prejudice, intolerance, and hatred. I feel I must continue talking as a memorial to those Six Million who cannot speak, so that the world will not forget and, it is hoped, will not let it happen again—anyplace—to anyone.

Let us not repeat the mistakes of fifty years ago, when most of the world looked away. The guilt is not Germany's alone. Some of it belongs to the silent bystanders as well.

In 1938 my Uncle Arnold, who had moved his family from Palestine to America in 1937, returned to Berlin. He was returning from a Swiss sanitarium where he had supposedly been treated for drug addiction. My aunt had hocked all her jewelry in what would prove to be a valiant, but vain, effort to cure her husband. During his Berlin detour, Arnold made an all-out effort to get me, my mother, *and my grandmother* out of the country. My uncle had a very congenial, persuasive way of talking to people. He could charm the birds off the trees.

Uncle Arnold took us to the American consul and *begged* him to place my mother and grandmother under the registration number to which I had already been assigned. The consul agreed to add my mother because I was too young to travel alone. But he adamantly refused to add my grandmother's name. Arnold begged and pleaded. The consul said he had never heard a man beg so much for his mother-in-law. Sadly, however, even though he had the power to grant us this seemingly small request—this small request that meant my grandmother's life—this United States government representative simply refused.

Return to Berlin, 1989

Berlin 1989. Fifty years after I left—with mixed emotions of sadness, uncertainty, anticipation, and joy in escaping the madness of the Nazi regime—I am returning, again with mixed emotions of anticipation, uncertainty, and sadness for all our loved ones who were lost, and even with some joy to be returning and renewing old memories.

I'm feeling much turmoil. At age sixty-eight, I will show my eighteen-year-old granddaughter Debbie the city where I was born, the places where I grew up, where I played as a child, where I spent most of my youth. Is she going to like it? Can she picture our life here so long ago?

Driving into the city from the airport is no different from arrivals anywhere else. As we approach the center of town, things begin to look familiar. Yes, this is still the city I left fifty years ago, not the one I visited in 1970, when it was still not back to normal. The only reminder of the war is the bombed-out steeple of Kaiser Wilhelm Memorial Church, left in ruins so that people will never forget—its modern addition now used for worship. Debbie's first observation, "It's so clean here!" Yet Berliners consider it dirty.

The hotel is in the center of my former neighborhood, across the street from the world-famous zoo, around the corner from Kurfürstendamm, with all the stores, movie houses, cafés, and one of the large department stores I remember so well. I can't wait to walk along the streets, breathe the Berlin air. I recall how often I thought, whenever I returned from a trip, "How special the air smells here!" How happy I always was to come home!

Debbie is tired from the long trip, so *I* start to explore. A few stores are still here, some even carry the names of their Jewish founders who were forced to sell them for almost nothing. Most of the old cafés have reopened. I walk around Kaiser Wilhelm Memorial Church, where I had walked the day before I left, and I remember watching the girls' skirts blowing in the breeze, thinking I would never see Berlin again. And here I am. It is like a dream. The city is exciting, alive, just as I remember it. Theaters, concerts, cabarets. It seems never to sleep.

My emotions are very mixed. I look at the people, most of whom are young. This is a city for the young, a fun place, and there is no conscription (in contrast to the rest of West Germany). I am thinking: "They had nothing to do with the Holocaust. They carry no guilt." But I also see the older people, and anger wells up. What was their role in the atrocities? Was that man a guard in a death camp? Was that woman one who cheered when we watched our Temple burn on Kristallnacht? All these thoughts race through my mind. What am I doing back here, filled with nostalgia? I have no answer.

Here's the little café where my grandmother and I spent so many happy hours, sipping coffee or hot chocolate with a delicious pastry. I think of her with love and gratitude, and I realize how she must have suffered during those last terrible years; how lonely she must have been with all of us gone. Sadness engulfs me.

I cross the street to the beautiful zoo, where my mother and her friends would have their afternoon coffee and play bridge in one of the garden restaurants while I was "parked" across the way in the playground.

Along the Kurfürstendamm were the movie houses where I spent many hours. I remember seeing *Naughty Marietta* three times. Next door I would buy a ticket for *San Francisco* when the sign clearly read, "No Jews Allowed." That never stopped me, and I was lucky not to have been caught.

Again, I ponder the question of why I feel at home after all these years. Why do I no longer hate? This is the city that deprived me of a normal youth, of everything and everyone I cared about, and sent me into exile. I rationalize, as always: *Berlin* is not Germany. The Berliners were different. And I think they still are. I do not have this feeling about the whole country. There is a new generation of Germans here now. We cannot blame them for the sins of their fathers, can we?

We ride the buses and subways everywhere. Timetables and routes are posted in every station, and schedules are punctual. The trains and stations are clean, exhibiting no graffitti. Nothing has changed in fifty years.

I visit the street where I was born. The house still stands. The entire street is untouched. I remember our large garden with tomato plants. I recall the trick I mentioned earlier, picking tomatoes, taking a bite out of each, and putting them back under the vines. I see a white bag filled with our breakfast rolls, hung there by the baker every morning. But I don't remember too much more; I was only three when we moved.

My school was in a suburb, and the buildings still stand. The entire estate had been commandeered by the then Foreign Minister, Joachim von Ribbentrop, for his private residence, forcing the school to close. The swimming pool has been filled in and is overgrown with grass. I can picture the beautiful grounds, with the pool, the running track, the tennis courts. How privileged we were to have attended such a school, with its excellent hand-picked teaching staff, all having been dismissed from German public schools. Teachers and pupils were a close-knit "family," sharing a common fate, concentrating on emigrating and surviving. How long ago—fifty years—and yet sometimes it feels as if it were only yesterday.

We visit the Jewish Community Center built on the site of one of the many synagogues burnt to the ground on that fateful night of November 1938. Only the portal remains standing, with the new Center built around it. Too many sad memories. I remember the beautiful synagogue so very well.

At the information center for Jewish affairs I am confronted with multiple volumes containing lists of the Jews of Berlin. I scan through them and find the names of most of my relatives, including my grandmother. All are captioned, *verschollen* (lost). It doesn't say "murdered," simply "lost."

All across the city are reminders of the Nazi years. People no longer shy away from exposing the events. There is an exhibition called "Topography of Terror," which re-creates the interrogation center, brick walls and all, that was the terror of everyone called there to be questioned and possibly tortured. It's there for all to see. The past is no longer hidden. Many visitors pass through. The young Germans demand to know what happened, how their elders could have allowed it to happen. There are some who say, "We don't want to hear about it anymore. We are not guilty. We had nothing to do with it." This I can also understand. In front of one of the subway stations I see a plaque with the names of all the concentration camps.

The pilgrimage into the past is only part of our visit, however. We do many fun things. We eat good food, with lots of sweets. The pastry is delicious, and so are the "Wieners" bought from a street vendor and eaten standing in the street. I savor the white asparagus I had longed for, and we eat apple strudel with warm vanilla sauce. We see *Porgy and Bess* in English, and we attend a concert at Philharmonic Hall, a very stark modern building.

When it is time to leave Berlin, I ask myself, "How does it feel to leave this time?" Not too bad. I think I will return soon. There are so many things left undone, places to see. I never got to the Jewish cemetery to visit the graves of my grandfather and my uncle. I must come back to sit in a sidewalk café, to see a cabaret, to go to the opera.

Could I ever live in Berlin again? I honestly do not know. But that question will never have to be answered because I could not voluntarily repeat the breakup of a family and move so far away from my daughters and granddaughters. I must admit that I felt very much at home in Berlin. In the last analysis, however, I know that Boston is my home and that I belong here now.

Giving Talks to Young People

For years, I have been speaking to students in public schools and colleges about my childhood experiences. This effort has been extremely gratifying. I have spoken to students at Wellesley College and Simmons College and to middle and high school students.

Young audiences like to hear what it was like to have grown up in Germany as a teenager during those years of Nazi turmoil. I usually encourage questions so that we can have a dialogue, which is always interesting for the students and for me.

I am asked many amazing questions, particularly by schoolchildren. One of the most common is: "Did you ever actually see Hitler in person?" And my response is "Yes, one day I saw him in Berlin, sitting in his car, which was stopped at a red light. I will never forget those piercing eyes peering at me through the windshield."

Why Do I Write?

"Why do you want to write?" was the first question asked when I enrolled in a writing class.

Why do I want to write? Do I have something worthwhile to say? Maybe so. Maybe someday my grandchildren will say, "Wow, she was quite a woman, this grandma of ours." On the other hand, I may only want to keep a diary, just for myself, to be destroyed, unread, after my death. And it must be in a style I can tolerate. That's why I would like to learn to write well, if one can learn such a thing.

My life, like that of most people, has been filled with agony and ecstasy. I have experienced the heights of joy and the depths of despair. I had to leave the country of my birth and all that was familiar and dear to me, to escape the fury of a mad dictator. I was more fortunate than many. I survived, though certainly not unscathed. No one could remain so under the circumstances. Most of my family were murdered in concentration camps. Adjustment to this country was difficult, but soon life became quite good, with the usual crises of marriage, rearing of children with measles, chicken pox, and all the other major and minor upsets, followed by the teenage years of broken and mended hearts and exciting and undying loves, never before experienced by anyone else! Show me a parent who has not lived through those years, doubting all the while that they would ever make it! But make it we did, to the surprise of no one but ourselves.

Now there is the pleasure of grandchildren who can be sent home when they become too rambunctious or become ill. Ah, the joy of being a grandmother, with all the pleasures and none of the worry, or so we think. I still worry along with their parents. Will they be all right? Will they escape the drug scene and the Krishna craze? And so it goes, on and on, from generation to generation, with laughter and tears and with hope, hope that there will be more joy than sadness in the final accounting. And finally we pray that we have instilled in them the strength to bear whatever life has in store for them.

Each Life Is Unique, and So Is Each Story

by Jean Kramer

Reprinted from the *Brookline Citizen*, June 18, 1987

Berlin, 1939: A young Jewish woman says farewell to the city of her birth, which she loves.

"On this, my last day in Berlin—a beautiful summer day in July—I walked down the Kurfürstendamm, the Fifth Avenue of Berlin, to the Kaiser Wilhelm Memorial Church [which would be bombed badly during the war], and as I watched young girls walking with their skirts flying in the breeze, my eyes brimmed over with tears, and I realized that this picture would be in my memory forever. This was the last time I would be walking along these streets.

"No matter how much we wanted to get out, no matter how much we had suffered during the last few years, the pain of parting and leaving everything and everyone I loved was almost unbearable. And I felt very much alone; I had no one with whom I could discuss these feelings. I could not cry to my friends who were unable to leave and who would be caught in the web when the war started one month later. And I certainly could not burden my poor grandmother, who had to stay behind.

"The next day, when my mother and I were ready to leave, I thought my heart would break. I will never forget the scene at the railroad station—there were so many people parting from their loved ones, so many tears—and my grandmother's face as she embraced us that last time will forever be etched in my memory."

When Irene Schlesinger Woods, herself a grandmother now, read from her autobiography at a recent presentation in the Brookline Library, many of her listeners felt tears in their own eyes. Nearly fifty years later, the aching beauty of things forever lost and the testimony of an individual caught up in momentous events could engage them personally in history and in the lives of others.

Mrs. Woods is a member of a seminar in autobiographical writing called "Telling Your Story," which has been meeting for the past two years under the sponsorship of the Brookline Adult and Community Education Program. The sixteen or so participants are older people whose ages range from sixty-five to nearly ninety, alike only in that each has the time and temperament to reflect on his or her own experiences and to make from them a statement. Some of these statements have been collected in a book to be published next fall and placed in the Brookline Public Library's archives of twentieth-century Brookline history.

Writers know about the power of autobiography. "This is my letter to the world," wrote Emily Dickinson, and John Cheever claimed, "I write to make sense of my life." Psychologists are beginning to recognize it as well. Dr. Kenneth Nobel, a psychiatrist who works with the elderly, has described the uses that older people make of the past to re-confirm themselves in the present. As an adolescent establishes an identity from the future and from what he may become then, so an older person uses past accomplishments and experience to reestablish that identity. As Irving Schwartz, who organized the seminar, observes, "Each life is unique; so is each life's story."

Local history, originally thought to be the focus for "Telling Your Story," has turned out to be the least of it. Each participant lives in this place at this time, but they have come together from all over the world and widely diverse backgrounds, bringing along both shared and unshared perspectives. One of them, David Bland, puts it thus: "With the telling of an incident by first one, then another, certain shadows began to stir, triggering forgotten events, people, times, and there you were—awakening sleeping moments and emotions. And by writing down these thoughts as if you were talking to someone else in the room—not composing, but simply thinking aloud—suddenly you found yourself writing with color, with harmony, with style."

David Bland continues, "I have always felt it was one of the final ironies of life that the memories each of us leaves for our children—and especially our grandchildren—are of someone feeble and old, a gentle soul perhaps, but not someone of distinction. Unknown to them is the sturdy youngster who strode forward as a youth as young as they, to struggle successfully with major events; perhaps to leave a homeland far away to come to a new country, with a new language, new culture, new customs; to survive depressions and wars; to create new lives to protect and support; to provide an education and a strong start in lives, their own lives.

"From time to time, talking to friends and relatives, I sometimes mention this autobiography group. Invariably, the response has been one of enthusiasm and great interest. It evokes immediate receptivity and identification, and eagerness to participate in similar groups, no matter where they live. Whether this promises an ego trip or expresses a very human desire to leave something personal to those behind us, I can't say; all I recognize is a universal need for whatever immortality may be captured in these dimming memories. I know that I express a hope all of us share that we can go on meeting together, sharing lives with former strangers, putting flesh and blood to shadows for the pleasure of grandchildren who may not yet be aware of their history but may, some day, be grateful to know more of us than a framed picture can ever reveal."

November 9 — A Significant Date — 1939-1989

The Berlin Wall

Reprinted from the *Brookline-Newton Tab*

My TV screen shows thousands of Berliners walking and shouting with joy as the wall and the barriers come tumbling down, and East and West interact happily. In my mind I see a different picture of another 9th of November, when Berliners were marching and shouting with joy as store fronts were smashed, synagogues were burning, and Jews were rounded up and beaten in the streets of the "Great" city of Berlin. No wall separated one section from the other then. The city and the people were united in brutality.

Fifty-one years ago! So much has happened since. Germany lost the war, the second one in twenty-five years, wars which she started. The country and the city of Berlin were divided into East and West at the end of World War II, occupied by the victors. The Berlin wall ran right through the middle of the city to remind people, and the world, of the atrocities committed by the German people and its elected government—to remind them of the havoc created in their name.

Now the country has come full circle. On this November 9, West Germany is one of the most successful and prosperous countries in Europe. Her economy is strong, thanks to the help of the United States, who put her on her feet after the war, but due also to the industry and ingenuity of her people. East and West are probably well on the road to unification and, God forbid, to becoming a world power again. Will it bode well or ill for her European neighbors? Will a "Greater Germany" be mindful of her past and remain a peaceful member of the world community, or will nationalism rise again and threaten the countries around her?

There are very personal thoughts churning around in my head. I was happy with a divided Germany because it represented for me some sense of justice, even of revenge, for the wrongs done to my family and my people. I felt it was right that those who had inflicted so much suffering on so many were suffering too, although there was no comparison to what the victims of German bestiality had experienced.

The reunification of Germany, however, brings me, on the one hand, to the realization that all is eventually forgiven, if not totally forgotten. On the other, watching the events near the Brandenburg Gate, nostalgia sets in once again. I recall the happy pre-1933 days, when Berlin was one wonderful city. I realize that this was so very long ago and that a new generation is now walking the streets without being stopped and searched. And it occurs to me that most of these young people are experiencing that freedom for the first time, having grown up in a divided city and a divided country. Will East and West mix? Will people who have lived in a controlled society be able to deal with the freedom, the abundance, the different values and, yes, also the decadence of the West? Will the forbidden fruit, no longer forbidden, taste as good in actuality as it had in imagination?

I am intrigued by these questions. Only time will tell. There is already some indication about the feelings of visitors from the East. Many of them, in interviews, make it clear that all they want to do is look and then return to their homes, that they have no intention of remaining. I am reminded of some Russians whom I recently met, who had no interest in leaving their country. I concluded that it was a very smart move by the Communist regime to allow people to travel freely to the West in the hope that they will return and help bring about changes in the East instead of running away.

The changes occurring all across Europe are heartening and confirm our belief that communism, as it has been practiced, cannot succeed in the long run. People will not be repressed forever. Everyone has a right to be free. It will be interesting to see how this freedom will be handled by the masses who have been oppressed for so long. I truly hope that democracy will prove to be a blessing for all who so fervently longed for it.

December 1989

The Summer of 1989 — Where Has It Gone?

I have written nothing all summer. Isn't it disgraceful to be loafing so totally and happily? That's the question I've been asking myself. Aside from a trip to California, I've stayed in the city, and it has been marvelous. There was so much to do. Boston is a pleasure in the

summer. All the students have left, and the city is relatively quiet, especially on weekends. I never venture out to where the tourists go. Quincy Market is out. But there have been some good plays, some movies and concerts for everybody's taste. I didn't even get to Tanglewood this summer. [Summer home of the Boston Symphony Orchestra.]

I have been greatly disturbed during the past few months. My own mortality is constantly facing me. My mother is almost ninety-two years old and my aunt is turning ninety. I hear the ever-recurring lament, "Why do we have to live so long?" The question occupies me often. I cannot escape the daily confrontation with old age, far beyond the point where life is still enjoyable. I watch her vision and hearing diminish daily. There is no hope for things to improve, they obviously will only worsen. And there is no answer, especially in the United States. If one is fortunate enough to live in a country like the Netherlands, for example, where euthanasia is legal, one has a choice—a doctor can help.

I am helpless, beyond listening to the sadness, the weeping, day in and day out. I am the caregiver and, in spite of the compassion I feel, I am often resentful. I am resentful because I've been cast in a role I do not want. I feel that at age sixty-eight I have earned the right to do as I please. I would like to have someone take care of me sometimes. I am tired. Tired of experiencing role reversal. I do not want to mother my mother. Yet she looks to me for answers, for constant support. On the other hand, she wants to know where I go every day, with whom, and why. I resent being questioned incessantly. I resent still having to answer to my mother.

It's a dilemma without a solution. I feel sorry for her, but at the same time I am angry because of the position I am forced into. I feel guilty when my patience wears thin and I blow up.

Will it ever end? Mothers making daughters feel guilty? My daughters have strict instructions to "shoot me" if I should ever do this to them. But in spite of their assurances that I'm "not like that," I am often afraid. Will my attitude be different? Will I have the fortitude and wisdom to be more accepting of old age with its frailties, its problems, its disabilities? I hope so, but who can tell?

The Reunification of Germany

Thinking people everywhere are being asked, "How do you feel about the reunification of Germany?" I have listened to radio and television commentators and to panel discussions by experts. I have read newspaper and magazine articles and editorials, all expressing divergent views and mixed feelings. There are citizens of bordering countries who view current events with alarm.

Some Americans are of the opinion that it is inevitable—that a divided Germany is unnatural. Many young Germans are concerned lest nationalism rear its menacing head once again. They understand the fears of Germany's neighbors.

Even Holocaust survivors are divided in their views. Though it has been fifty years, some will never forget. However, a new generation now lives in Germany—a generation that wishes to enjoy peace with its neighbors and make amends for the crimes of their parents and grandparents. I have recently spoken with many of these young people. Most are quite emphatic about their stance. Many have no nationalistic feelings. They consider themselves citizens of the world. They are not interested in a "Greater Germany," but are looking for peace and prosperity—in that order—and for contact with their peers in Europe and beyond.

Germans, as a whole, are confused and unsure whether unification will be healthy for both East and West. West Germans fear that the help that is required of them will undercut their capital and comfort. They are aware of the deep-seated differences between the life styles, experiences, and economies of East and West. East Germans fear being swallowed by the prosperous, savvy West, that their values will nosedive in the race for the almighty dollar, i.e., mark. The violence shown on our television and movie screens daily will surely be exported to the East, where censorship has not permitted such films to be shown for more than forty years. They are concerned that once the restrictions are lifted, their crime rate will rise, their young will be corrupted, and drug use will become rampant. They are worried that their kinder, gentler, more helpful attitude—dictated by necessity, to be sure—will disappear as soon as their economic situation improves. I am reminded of the "kinder, gentler nation" I came to in 1939, before prosperity

increased. It seems that as the level of prosperity rises, the level of humanity decreases. Someone recently posed the question, "Is there such a thing as prosperity with a human face?"

My personal feeling is not one of alarm at the prospect of German reunification. I have great faith in the young people who are the future. I worry only about the flag wavers, who are still dreaming of "Deutschland Uber Alles" (Germany Above Everything). Fortunately, at this writing, they are in the minority. As I see it, Germany is becoming a great power through her economic success.

Along with many other people, I believe that, due to their diligence and work ethic, Germany and Japan will be the superpowers of the twenty-first century. We here in the United States are sadly lagging. Our economy is in shambles, starting at the government level, and we live beyond our means. Banks are folding and businesses are declaring bankruptcy or are being taken over by Japan. Our educational system has broken down. Our children are growing up ignorant, poorly educated, pushing and using drugs, carrying guns and knives to school, unable to compete with students in other advanced nations. All the while they seem not to care. Our work ethic is deplorable. Few take pride in a job well done or care about their neighbor.

We are one of the few civilized countries without national health insurance. Crime is out of control. The number of poor and homeless in this land of plenty is increasing. And all we do is blame everyone but ourselves. One reason why I am not worried about Germany starting another war is that I anticipate that Germany and Japan will soon divide the world between them because their workers are diligent and hardworking. They take pride in their work and they have a tremendous urge to succeed. Someday, we may wake up to find that we have been asleep and have been taken over without a shot being fired. I believe that it would be well for us to become vigilant and try to overhaul our lax society, lest we end up a satellite of Germany and Japan.

Spring 1990: A Journey Through the Past — and the Present

Vienna. City of Mozart and Strauss. City of Waldheim and Nazi collaborators. Those were my thoughts as I stepped out onto the street from the airport. Riding through the streets, however, I could not help being impressed by the beautiful old buildings, the parks with manicured lawns and abundant flowers, the cleanliness of sidewalks and roadways. People walked unhurriedly. Outdoor cafés were crowded. A mood of peace and quiet prevailed. No boom boxes, no blaring radios. Even teenagers acted civilized. I wondered why it couldn't be like that back home in the U.S.A.?

Like so many places in Austria, our hotel still bore the K & K (Kaiserlich/Koeniglich) insignia. It seemed that the people were clinging to nostalgia for their royal family. Statues and pictures of the old Emperor, Franz Josef, and of other members of royalty were ubiquitous—a kind of culture lag of 100 years.

We inspected the city quite thoroughly in the few short days of our visit. As in most European cities, public transportation is efficient, modern, clean, and punctual. There were no tickets available for cultural events or for a performance of the famous Lippizzaner horses. This was festival week in Vienna, and all performances had been sold out months in advance.

Unlike Germans, Austrians do not have many reminders of the Hitler years. There is a Resistance Museum, but it was closed on the day of our visit. There is an impressive memorial to the "victims of the Gestapo" on the site of the former Gestapo headquarters which, I was told, had been in one of Vienna's best hotels.

After many inquiries, we found the Jewish cemetery. My traveling companion grew up in Vienna. His sister had died there in 1925 at age nineteen. To locate her grave, we had to sift through an enormous card file provided by the administrator, who told us a harrowing tale of the murder of his young wife, shot while trying to shield a child during a terrorist attack on the synagogue a few years ago. Incredulous, I asked him how he could bear to remain in Vienna. In spite of his admission of rampant anti-Semitism in Austria, he claimed not to have any other alternative. Remarried, and with a young family, he must earn a living. My question "What about Israel?" was met with an emphatic "No" from this ultra-orthodox Jew. I was stunned—and disgusted.

Walking through the cemetery was a wrenching experience, not only because of my friend's emotional confrontation with the past at the grave of his sister, but also because we came face to face with the history of the Jewish people etched on many of the headstones. They told the story of the dispersion of European Jewry. Many carried the names of entire families killed during the Holocaust, or the names of survivors living all over the world: from Sao Paulo to Haifa and New

York to Australia. Confronted with the story of our people, we asked ourselves, "Will it ever end?" Then we saw new graves, new names added recently, and I wondered what prompted some Jews to return, or to stay after being in hiding during the war, having witnessed the brutality heaped on the Jews. This question was on my mind often during this visit, especially in Munich and Berlin.

Walking slowly toward the cemetery exit, we reflected on our lives, our experiences, our personal tragedies, and the tragedy of our people. We thought with sadness of all those who perished, with revulsion at the ones who committed the unthinkable crimes, and with anger toward those who stood by and let it all happen.

We spent the next few days strolling through the streets and parks of this charming city. I fell in love with it, pushing away all thoughts of the past. I enjoyed the good food. No one seemed to worry about cholesterol, and I decided to "assimilate." It was wonderful. Looking around, I concluded that there were fewer fat people here than at home. I was less delighted with the excessive smoking we encountered throughout Europe, and I wondered if they knew something we did not. Compared to ours, what is their death rate from cancer or heart disease?

When it was time to leave, after much too brief a stay, I did so regretfully.

On the way to the train station we were fortunate, or unfortunate, to be driven by a very gabby cabby, who felt compelled to tell us all about the "new" Austria. "Society is going to hell, the economy is declining, everyone is buying on credit, as if they didn't have to pay the piper in the end, no one is saving one schilling," and on and on. It sounded to me as if the American way had spread to this part of the world, too, and the cabby didn't like its Austrian imitators.

Our train ride to Salzburg was a joy. The train was spotless, quiet, and fast. We traveled through the picturesque countryside, unfortunately in pouring rain, which continued until our arrival. We were told that "it always rains in Salzburg." Terrific beginning! However, the town is so charming that nothing could dampen our spirits, not even the pelting rain. Walking on cobblestones may be quaint, but it is certainly hard on shoes and feet.

Munich was a different experience entirely. Our hotel was in the middle of a completely Turkish neighborhood. Everyone had an accent, including the chambermaids. All I could think of was that Hitler would turn over in his grave, seeing what has happened to his "Aryan" nation. One had the feeling of being in one of the Mediterranean countries. Men were sitting at tables in the street, playing cards, drinking. What an "un-German" way of life!

We took the subway to the opera house to buy tickets for *Don Giovanni*, arriving at 6:02 P.M. The box office had closed at 6:00 sharp. German order! We did manage to get tickets for *La Traviata* and saw a first-class performance. The next day we took a city tour, including the Olympic Stadium. Thoughts of the 1972 terrorist attack on the Israeli athletes haunted me. There seemed to be no escape from the painful memories.

Munich is a clean, attractive city, much of it rebuilt after the war. Clean, efficient public transportation took us everywhere. Escalators do not waste energy by running constantly. They start when someone steps onto them.

After much reflection, we decided to go to Dachau. Neither of us had ever wanted to visit the camps. But being so close, not having known anyone who perished there, we thought we would be able to bear it. The experience was overwhelming. To actually stand in front of the cremation ovens, the gas chamber that had never been used, to enter the barracks, watch a film, and walk through the extensive, starkly impressive exhibition was emotionally draining. But I do not regret having seen with my own eyes this evidence of man's inhumanity to man.

Traveling back to the subway station through this picturesque little town, we kept thinking back to fifty years ago, when the cattle cars were rattling through the town day in and day out. I asked myself how it was possible that people did not know what was happening, as many have claimed. How had that huge complex, ringed with barbed wire, the clearly visible watch towers, existed in this small town without people being aware of what was taking place here? Anger welled up in me, and I realized why I cannot talk to Germans my age and older without thinking, "What did you do during the Hitler years and during the war?" I feel no animosity toward any of the young Germans. They are not guilty, and I do not believe we can hold them responsible for the crimes of their elders.

The remainder of our stay was spent sightseeing in Munich and vicinity.

Last stop: Berlin. A city bus took us from the airport almost to the door of our hotel for a fare of $1.50. In spite of my good intentions, I felt nostalgic. Part of the city looked very much as it had fifty years ago. Our hotel was right on Kurfürstendamm. Breathing Berlin air, gas fumes and all, reminded me of the days when I used to arrive here happily from wherever I had been, always glad to be "home." I kept telling myself that this is no longer my home. Now I am only a visitor. We were close to my old neighborhood, and I loved it. We dropped our luggage at the hotel and strolled down Kurfürstendamm, lined with fine shops and an abundance of inviting outdoor cafés, crowded with people. Our first stop was a ticket agency, to make sure that we would be able to attend some of the numerous cultural and not-so-cultural offerings. We decided on a cabaret (Berlin was always full of political cabarets) and on a performance of *Carmina Burana,* one of my favorites, at the Berliner Staatsoper in East Berlin. Many of the cultural events take place in that part of the city, and some of the best museums are located there, including the impressive Pergamon Museum, where the great Pergamon altar has been reassembled. I remembered it so well from our school trips and how my interest had been dampened then by the certain knowledge that the next day we would have to write a composition about everything we had seen. Ugh!

I made a few phone calls to round up all my friends. Three of my young German "pals" visited in the evening and took us "drinking" at the Literary Café, in the building of a fine bookstore, with a garden café. Most of the drinking was done by them, of course. I had my favorite, "Berliner Weisse," a mixture of wine, seltzer, and raspberry syrup. The young people filled us in on the political situation, the fall of the wall, the excitement of it all. The next morning, one of the boys took us on a tour of the city.

We drove through the old familiar streets and noted the many new buildings, next to the old ones. I realized then how much of the city had been destroyed by Allied bombs. Was there some justice, after all? Some of the old buildings still carry the scars of the air raids. I recognized many of the streets. Several had been renamed after the war. At the site of one of the old synagogues, which had been used as a collection center for Jews to be shipped to extermination camps, a Holocaust Memorial had been constructed. On the sidewalks were rails leading to the replica of an old cattle car, underneath which figures sculpted from gray marble were huddled. In back of this car was another marble sculpture, depicting a group of figures huddled and tied together with an iron cable, signifying the way people were "shipped" like packages.

Behind this group rose a tall sheet of rusty metal with a long list of dates and destinations of the sixty-three transports that had left from here. On one of the remaining walls of the old synagogue a plaque contained the story of this memorial. On one side of the cattle car the entire sidewalk was covered with bronze plaques showing all the synagogues of Berlin, the dates they were first burned, the dates they were bombed, and finally when they had to be destroyed completely. I recognized the two we had attended and was overcome with a tremendous feeling of sadness and loss.

I also acknowledged the fact that here at least was an attempt to keep this unspeakable tragedy alive in people's memory.

We next drove to East Berlin. Although the wall had been torn down, we still had to pass through Checkpoint Charlie. With only one week left before this famous (or infamous, whichever way you looked at it) wall would be removed, the East Germans were happy to collect DM5.00 per person for a few more days. Crossing into East Berlin was like entering another country. Very few buildings had been restored. Ruins were everywhere, and nothing was kept up very well. Christian, our guide, took us to the old Jewish Quarter, where I had never been. He showed us the oldest Jewish cemetery in the area. The only gravestone still standing is the one on the grave of Moses Mendelssohn. All the others have been removed, ostensibly to have them restored.

At the entrance there is a monument showing a group of bedraggled people. Survivors! A plaque inscription noted that this was the site of an old-age home and that seventy-three transports had left from here.

Around the corner were the remnants of one of the most beautiful synagogues in Europe. Only the facade was still standing. Christian told us that it was finally going to be restructured into a museum. The scaffolding had been there for a long time. East Germans don't work too quickly. I suppose that all this will change after unification has been achieved.

At this point, we needed a change of pace, a change of mood, and so we decided to have lunch at one of the best restaurants in East Berlin. The price was about one-third of what it would have been in the West. Service was poor, as in most places in the East. The prices will undoubtedly triple after unification. I fear that the East Germans will have a rude awakening—in many ways.

Our last stop on that day was the Jewish cemetery. I wanted to visit the graves of my grandfather and my uncle, who had died at age nineteen after World War I. It was sad to see the beautiful old cemetery neglected, overgrown with ivy. I was surprised, however, to see that most of the gravestones were still standing. Not many were destroyed or overturned, as I had expected. My grandfather's stone was intact, and Antonia, one of our old employees, had had my grandmother's name added, with the inscription "Murdered in Auschwitz in 1944." I was gripped with emotion and remembered gratefully this loyal old woman for her kind gesture. Unfortunately, due to shoddy East German workmanship, the added letters were crumbling and would have to be reset. The ones affixed in 1935 are in perfect condition. Christian promised to clean the graves and put them in order. Another indication that there are some good Germans!

Walking along the pathways, we observed the same sad story of the dispersion of Jews throughout the world and of the many killed during

Gravestone of Adolf Pelz; Jenny's name added by Antonia after the war

the Holocaust. Again, we saw new graves—and the same question was in our minds: "How many Jews came back, how many survived here? What was it like to live here?"

One of my former girlfriends had lived in Berlin through the war years. Both she and her husband are half-Jewish, having had one non-Jewish parent. She was put in a concentration camp for a short while, but her Christian mother managed to have her released. I was told that this was not uncommon. The rest of the time they lived illegally, without papers. No one wanted to talk about those years, and I was reluctant to ask, realizing what a painful experience it must have been, one not easily recalled even after all this time.

Concluding this exhausting day, we needed some relief, which we got at the cabaret. The Berliners' famous sense of humor was still intact, and it was a thoroughly enjoyable evening, even though it was sometimes difficult, even for me, to follow the fast talking.

The next morning was spent at the old Reichstag (parliament) which was set on fire in 1933. A poor, feeble-minded Dutchman was executed for a crime he could never have committed. The building had been restored, and city government and parliament, I believe, still meet there. After unification it will undoubtedly be restored to its former glory and will be the seat of a new German government. It houses a fine exhibition of the history of Germany. We ate at one of its excellent restaurants.

In the evening, back across Checkpoint Charlie with the same red tape, to the Staatsoper (State Opera). Here was a building in East Berlin that had been restored to its former beauty. I remembered how often I had been here as a young girl. We saw an excellent performance of *Carmina Burana*. Afterward we strolled down "Unter den Linden," one of the beautiful boulevards of old Berlin. We had coffee and cake in one of the many restaurants along the avenue. I could easily get fat here, I thought.

Surprisingly, East Berlin was quite lively, almost as much as the other side, where the city never sleeps, where people seem to be up and about all night. I fondly remembered the many times I visited my grandfather in his office, here on Unter den Linden, so many years ago. How scared I used to be when I had to get on or off the "Pater Noster" elevator. I am sure it was perfectly safe because it was in operation for many years. Nevertheless, it was quite frightening for a little girl with short legs.

On our last day in Berlin, in pouring rain, we criss-crossed the city by subway, by bus and on foot. I guess I was saying good-bye again!

We met a young Russian family for afternoon coffee—friends of friends in Boston. They had lived in Berlin for the past ten years and professed to love it. The husband told us that as a physician he was making a very good living, taking vacations four times a year. Their life, they said, was wonderful, but they know that they will always be considered foreigners in Germany. I realized that not much has changed in that respect. I had expected to hear of their experiencing anti-Semitism, but not of this old prejudice against foreigners. I again asked myself, why would young Jews want to bring up their children in such an atmosphere? Here are people with close family in Israel. Why? I concluded that money must be terribly important to them and I was quite disillusioned.

We walked to the Jewish community center, built on the site of one of the old synagogues that was destroyed during Kristallnacht. All that was left standing was the portal with two columns, and the center has been built around this imposing entrance. In my mind, I could still visualize the synagogue. How magnificent it had been so long ago.

The bus took us to the airport. I was sorry to leave. The trip was too short. There are still many places left to visit and too many things left to do. I guess I'll have to return again soon.

My Daughter Myra's Farewell to My Mother

January 7, 1991

We have come together today to say good-bye to my grandmother, who lived a very full life and died at age ninety-three. Instead of reciting a historical chronology of her life, I would like to share with all of you, her friends and family, my remembrances and personal feelings about her and her role in our family.

I have fading yet fond memories of my early childhood visits to her house—Oriental rugs, overstuffed furniture, and heavily framed still-life paintings. Also, staying up late and being treated to applications of brightly colored fingernail and toenail polish—how grown up I felt! Although late bedtimes and nail polish for young children were strongly vetoed by my mother, they were requests mischievously granted by my grandmother as our very own secret. And how can I forget a kitchen equipped with contraptions providing endless entertainment and activity—an appliance for mechanically grinding bread crumbs, a washing machine with a hand-wringer, and an elaborate system of weights and balances, all designed to delight curious eyes and hands.

Throughout my teens and early adulthood, visits dwindled. I was much too busy studying, much too busy shopping, much too busy partying, much too busy traveling, much too busy working, much too busy marrying, and much too busy, period.

It was not until my grandmother's last years that my visits again increased, and I came to know her at all. She was a woman of many contradictions. Often stubborn, often indecisive, often demanding, she was also always sociable, always eager to hear "what else is new," always delighted to receive visits from you, her friends, always willing to discuss her views of the world, always welcoming the opportunity to reminisce about her younger years in Germany, the transition to this country, and her many travel adventures. She displayed a fierce loyalty to her family and friends and, despite her failing health, maintained an incredible will to remain independent and in control of both her body and mind. Although no one else seemed to mind, she chastised herself for her faulty memory and failing eyesight and hearing. Even when frail and in pain, she pushed herself to get out of bed and take a short walk each day in order to keep herself mobile. At age eighty-eight she successfully weathered major surgery. She was truly remarkable.

No discussion of my grandmother's later years can exclude acknowledgment of my mother Irene, her daughter and only child. Often under difficult circumstances, my mother accepted the challenge of ensuring that my grandmother's physical and emotional needs were well met. As a senior citizen herself, my mother still singlehandedly researched residential facilities, engineered the move to North Hill, acted as an advocate with staff, managed all financial affairs, telephoned daily, visited weekly, organized birthday and holiday celebrations, scheduled doctors' visits, interviewed and hired companions—the list goes on and on. In countless ways, both big and small, she rearranged her own priorities to accommodate my grandmother's needs. Who could ask more from a daughter?

And who can ever repay the endless kindnesses extended to my grandmother and my family by all the staff at North Hill, and by her extended family, Barbara and Peggy? Every day they went beyond their job descriptions.

Members of a family are forever interwoven, and all families experience a void when a member dies. My grandmother's absence will be felt by her daughter Irene, her sister Ruth Meyer (at age ninety-one, unable to be here today), her two granddaughters, and her two great-granddaughters. But what a marvelous legacy. Stamina, curiosity, determination, loyalty, longevity, and love have been passed down from my grandmother and Aunt Ruth to my mother, my sister, and myself, and hopefully to my nieces Jennifer and Deborah. I am grateful to them all for the combined role model of strong, energetic, independent women whom they have provided me. These qualities are the ones I will remember most about my grandmother and her contribution to our family.

It is sad to say good-bye, but my grandmother is now free of pain and struggle and is today surrounded by family, friends, and flowers—she would be pleased.

My mother: Erna Summerfield

Sad Thoughts — January 23, 1991

My mother died last week. The struggle has ended. There was no opportunity for last words of love or of understanding. I was away and did not get home until it was too late. She was semiconscious and seemed not to know that I was there. My daughters had decided not to call me home earlier because she had always rallied before. They did what they thought was right.

Would it have made any difference? I doubt it. What could we have said to each other that we had not tried to say so many times before? She had wanted to tell me something before I left "in case we don't see each other again." She may have had a premonition, but she said this every time I left. As I remember now, it was something of no importance and—again—all the years of misunderstanding, lack of communication, hurt feelings certainly could not have been wiped out in those last short moments.

When I returned two days before she died and saw the change that had occurred in the short time I had been away, my heart went out to her, and I felt pain and regret that our relationship could not have been better. Suddenly, there was a moment of recognition, and the only words I heard were: "You do know where my money is, don't you?" I realized, again, what was most important to her. I was not angry any longer. I felt only sadness. I thought of a life never really lived to the fullest. Her preoccupation with money and things crowded out the feeling of warmth and satisfaction that comes from being a giving, caring human being. The joy of giving, of loving, and being loved is, in my view, the essence of a life well lived.

Mother-and-daughter is a primal relationship, and everyone's expectation is that there has to be love. But I have seen more strife and unhappiness emanating from this myth of mother love than from almost any other misconception. Enough books have been written on the subject to fill a very large bookcase. If mothers and daughters could only let go, accept their differences more honestly, learn to respect each other's shortcomings, cease trying to reach the impossible goal of a perfect relationship, much heartache could be avoided.

Yes, I think of my mother quite often. I find myself looking at the clock at nine in the morning, imagining that I should call her, as I always did at that hour, and sometimes when I got home in the afternoon, wanting to check if she's all right. Of course, the guilt is there, although I know that I did my very best, especially in the last years. Calling twice a day, visiting every weekend, more often if she needed me even though she was well cared for, was all that any daughter could have done.

Do I have regrets? Of course I do. I often ask myself, as I have done over the years, "Could I have been nicer, could I have overlooked more, could I have curbed my reactions and ignored the constant provocations? Should I have stopped taking the bait and avoided getting into any discussion every time she wanted an argument to satisfy her need for combat?" I know that I tried, but I also know that most of the time I failed.

I learned, to my amazement, that many people at North Hill, where she lived, were very fond of her. They got a kick out of her love for sparring. I have spoken to the few of her friends who are still around and have received notes from some of them. Everyone of them agrees that she was a good friend and a worthy opponent, but that she could be trying and aggravating as well. But they all miss her. They have lost a partner in combat. She always presented a challenge. The battles had held them together for so many years. Her sister Ruth, age ninety-one, tells me that she misses my mother, although they never got along too well, either. And from the beautiful eulogy my daughter Myra gave, I gathered that there was more than I thought to the grandmother aspect. It made me happy and blunted somewhat my hurt at the reaction I got when I told my mother so many years ago that she was going to have a grandchild. The first words I heard in response to my joyful news was "How can you afford to have a child?"

To everyone, the staff and some of the residents at North Hill, to her old friends, sometimes even to my daughters, she was a phenomenon—a spunky old lady who loved a good fight. To them she was a constant source of wonder, to have so much spirit at ninety-three. To me, she was my mother who had done very little mothering, had rejected me when I needed her, and had enjoyed combat all her life, whereas I shied away from it whenever I could. Yes, I give her credit for the spunk she displayed almost to the end, but the tug-of-war wore me out.

I still find it painful to remember the terrible frustration she felt about her advancing blindness. I marvel at how she never stopped clutching at every possibility for improvement, going so far as writing to Bob Hope, who also suffered from macular degeneration, requesting the name of his doctor. Maybe he could help her? Her tenacity was to be admired. Yet when all avenues were exhausted, and she was assured that there was nothing more anyone could do, she refused to accept the reality. She continued to fight, railing against the finality of blindness. This inability or unwillingness to deal with the inevitable made life so much more difficult for her and for everyone around her.

And yet, up to her last conscious moment, she cared about her appearance. She never failed to put on some jewelry when she went to the dining room, in spite of needing help to put on earrings, necklaces, etc. She never forgot the little dab of toilet water. She remained inquisitive and interested in everything that went on around her. I will never forget how, during our last telephone conversation when I called her from out-of-town, she told me that she hoped not to have to live through another war. She died on January 17 and the [Gulf] war, I believe, began on the following day. Her wish was granted.

As time passes, memories become kinder, more positive. I found some of her travel diaries and was surprised at what she wrote about, the sites she had seen, the experiences she had had. I thought about how, in her late seventies, she went down to the harbor and stood in line to tour the *J. F. Kennedy* aircraft carrier. I heard about this from a friend, never from her. She told me little of her interests, of her activities, just as I avoided telling her of mine because I feared the painful criticism.

What a great loss it was for both of us that we could not communicate. We never really knew each other. The eternal optimist in me had always hoped that our relationship would improve. But no matter how hard I tried, I could not bring about a change in her attitude. Now there is no longer a chance to make it right. I know that as a child I started out loving her, but as long as I can remember there never was any response. I trust that eventually the bad memories will fade and good ones will rise to the surface.

I hope that, wherever she is, she has found a sparring partner.

Irene's Enchanted Evening — March 24, 1991

The 24th of March is a date I will always remember. That night we celebrated a unique event: My seventieth birthday.

How clever of me to invite my large circle of family and friends to tell me and one another how wonderful I am! I was not in any way disappointed. It was such a pleasure hearing those completely candid and absolutely delicious words of appreciation, friendship, and love, words ordinarily left unuttered until we are no longer around to hear and enjoy them.

That evening, such words were spoken to an assembly of just about everyone I care about and who, I hope, cares about me.

"Young" people of all ages, seventeen to ninety-one, were present. Admiring friends and loving relatives, born in Berlin, Munich, Budapest, Vienna, England, Moscow, Leningrad—a truly international mishmash were in attendance. Even a few native-born Americans were sprinkled about—notably my daughters, their husbands, and mothers-in-law. Absent and sorely missed by me, and probably their other grandmother, were my granddaughters Jennifer and Debbie, whom duty prevented from attending.

My ninety-one-year-old Aunt Ruth made the trip from Cleveland, along with my cousins. For a year she had been talking of her hope to be in Boston for my big day. We spoke of how much my mother would have enjoyed being with us.

A former Berlin schoolmate came from New York to recall the days of our childhood and youth more than fifty years earlier.

Toasts were proposed, and some of my friends read amusing poems. But the highlight of the evening was the "unveiling" by Bunny and Myra, my dearest daughters, of the presentation they had planned and hinted at for the past year. It was a plaque signifying that my name and that of their father, Egon, had been inscribed on the "Immigrants' Wall of Honor" at Ellis Island. Although we had not entered America through that gateway, I was deeply touched by the thoughtfulness of this recognition.

I was also given a beautiful album containing the certificates and photographs taken by a friend of the island and its environs. These included the Statue of Liberty, the famous Manhattan skyline, some enormously impressive sculptures of a group of immigrants, and the wall showing our names.

This deeply gratifying surprise had been in the planning process for two years, and everyone involved prayed that I wouldn't be hit by a truck before March 24th.

Fat chance! I had my planso too. Little did they know that I intend to stick around for at least another thirty years to haunt my offspring.

The climax of the evening was the following tribute composed and delivered by my daughters.

March 24, 1991

Mom,

Today your family and friends are here to celebrate your seventieth birthday and express our love, admiration, and respect.

Many people reach seventy, which is still considered young, but not many lead as active or full a life as you.

• You've traveled to Russia, China, Israel, and Europe.

• You've written touching pieces in your autobiographical writing class.

• You are an enthusiastic theater and symphony goer.

• You've befriended and nurtured Russian immigrants.

• You are the No. 1 contributor to the Boston Globe Letters-to-the-Editor.

• You've been known to bid a slam correctly.

• And, of course, who can forget those daily walks!

One day we think you'll have to retire from "retirement!" In deciding how to honor you, we wanted to acknowledge both the happy life you prematurely left behind in Germany in 1939, and the rich life which you subsequently built in America.

Actually, you yourself supplied us with the kernel of an idea for a fitting tribute. We know of your ongoing interest in passing on awareness of the Holocaust, both through your lectures to school-children, and your recent donation of family memorabilia to the Holocaust Museum in Washington, D.C. In that way, you became a part of the dark history of Nazi Germany. We also wanted to commemorate the bright side, your entry into a new life in America, so that future generations would always be aware of that happy occasion.

So, instead of the bronzed Bloomingdale's Shopping Bag which came to mind, we'd like to present you with this certificate, which signifies that a plaque has been inscribed on the Immigrant Wall of Honor at Ellis Island with your name and Daddy's name.

We love you and value what you've shared with us as a mother and grandmother and friend. We hope to celebrate many, many more happy and healthy and active birthdays with you.

Love,

Michael and Bunny
Jeff and Myra
Jennifer and Debbie

From start to finish that evening was among my most lovely experiences, and I am very grateful to everyone who participated. It was an evening to linger over again and again in sentimental recollection.

Israel — October 1991

It is difficult to express my feelings and impressions of the scenes and sounds of my recent trip to Israel. How the country has changed since my first visit twenty years ago. So many developments, new buildings, archaeological excavations, monuments, and discoveries have come into existence. The progress of this small country, despite all the obstacles, is astonishing. I try to understand, and excuse, the nervousness, the loudness, the belligerence, the lack of courtesy among a people constantly living with the threat of attack, death, and disaster.

While we were there, an Arab deliberately drove his car into a queue of Israeli soldiers waiting for a bus, killing or injuring a number of them. The Hezbollah proudly claimed "credit" for this atrocity.

We look at the handsome young people and cannot shake the thought of the danger they constantly face. Will it ever end?

James Baker is in Jerusalem at the King David Hotel. Security is tight, police and military are very visible in the streets and on the rooftops surrounding the hotel. To enter, one must pass through metal detectors and show identification. A platform has been erected in the center of the lobby. Cameras are set up, the press is swarming everywhere for a press conference—in vain, as it turns out.

No one is optimistic that anything positive will come of the long-awaited peace conference. The PLO involvement is obvious, and will prompt the Israelis to walk out. Terrorist acts continue. Syria refuses to sit down with Israel to discuss the water problems of the region, but plans to attend the peace conference hoping to win the return of the Golan Heights as an "attendance prize." Everyone who has ever stood on the Golan Heights knows that it would be suicide for Israel to return this vital territory. In the valley below, bunkers are still visible where Israelis slept every night while the Syrians shelled the lowlands from above. So it goes, on and on, leading nowhere.

We observe the beautiful Arab children at play—not remarkably different from the Jewish children at the kibbutz we visited earlier that day. We see how all children play the same games. We look at those innocent faces and feel like weeping, realizing that it won't be long before they have learned well the lessons they are being carefully taught: to hate.

We drive through the arid desert with rare scattered patches of trees and vegetation, past Bedouin tents set up on barren hills, past Kibbutz Ein Gedi, an oasis with palm trees, houses, and fields. We arrive at Masada. We ride up in the cable car, then climb eighty steps to the fortress built by Herod, overlooking the Dead Sea. We hear again the now-familiar story of a small band of Jews who, eighteen centuries ago, held off an army of Romans for years, finally committing mass suicide rather than fall into the enemy's hands. The recital is intended to fill us with admiration and pride.

We visit Yad Vashem, the Memorial to the Six Million. There have been additions since I was there in 1970, notably the Children's Pavilion. It is indescribably moving and distressing. We enter a large building almost completely dark inside, feeling our way by holding onto a railing. All we see is smoked glass with small light bulbs scattered throughout, and then we hear the voices: voices calling out names; names of innocent children and the countries they had come from. When we emerge from this exhibit, no one is able to speak.

The hall with the names of all the concentration camps and the eternal flame in the center affected me as it did the first time I saw it. I was unable to remain, it was too much to bear. The adjoining museum, which houses pictures and documents of the years leading up to and encompassing the nearly total annihilation of European Jewry, evoked sorrow and anger. When we looked at the pictures of destruction and inhumanity, pictures we had seen so many times before, we had only one thought: no one even remotely connected with these unspeakable crimes should have been allowed to go on living. Everyone involved should have been executed. Prominently displayed in one of the glass cases are the notices repatriating two outstanding German Jews: Albert Einstein and Martin Buber.

On the second floor of the museum there is a file room where names of known Holocaust victims are in the process of being entered into computers to be inscribed in memory forever. Months ago, I had sent a list of members of my own family who had perished in Auschwitz, including my grandmother, two cousins, aunts and uncles.

I checked to see if my papers had been received and was shown copies of the list. But I was told that entering names into the computers would take some time. The museum was severely underfunded and understaffed. I thought that as long as the names were documented, it does not matter how long it will take to have them entered. My hope is that some day my daughters and granddaughters and generations still to come may visit Yad Vashem and find evidence of the tragic end of much of our family—people they were never privileged to know and love—whose love and warmth they had been deprived of.

Leaving the museum, we walk along the Street of the Righteous, named for the courageous Christians who helped Jews survive by hiding them or making it possible for them to escape—at enormous risk to themselves. Those brave souls are remembered with gratitude. May it ever be so!

Silently we leave, each with our own thoughts. I ponder the question: How do the Germans, who come through here in droves, deal with it all? During our two-week visit we noted, with some surprise, how many Germans were touring Israel. We spoke to several of the young people, wondering—but not actually asking, due to lack of opportunity—how they felt, seeing what their countrymen had done to other human beings. How many of their parents and grandparents had been involved? Had they been told what had happened?

There is so much more to say about this bittersweet journey, but I feel that, for now, I have said enough.

German-Jewish Dialogue

Who could have foreseen that such a group would ever be formed? How did we, Jews and Germans, get together to try to sort out, understand, forgive what certainly was the blackest period in both our histories?

Here we are, young, middle-aged, and older men and women—Jews and Germans: I am the only survivor in the group, which includes some American Jews and a rabbi, old enough to remember. Our group consists mostly of young and middle-aged children of survivors, members of an organization called "One Generation After." The other segment of our group is comprised of young and middle-aged Germans, members of the diplomatic corps, and young college students, eager to find out, in depth, what happened, how we now feel about them. They were born during or after the Nazi years, but still feel guilt for the horrors their parents and grandparents inflicted on others. They also feel ashamed for their country.

Where do we begin? Can we forgive? Can we talk to them without anger? There are awkward moments, awkward pauses. I, the only one who lived under the Nazi regime for six years, but who also grew up in the pre-Hitler Germany I loved, am more ready to understand and absolve this new generation of guilt than are the children of survivors. They are much less forgiving.

I have been asking myself, Why? I have not come up with a definite answer except, possibly, that these young people did not know Germany before it was engulfed in madness. They have no memory, as I have, of a better life and a better country. They can only deal with Germany and Germans as Holocaust perpetrators. I do not excuse or minimize, but I cannot lay blame on this new generation, who are the ages of my children and grandchildren and, in my view, bear no responsibility for the sins of their fathers. I do feel an instant rapport with them, born of my German background that I cannot deny and, which to this day, still lingers in my heart. I can talk easily with them. I speak their language and they speak mine. Their background is similar to mine. I do not, however, feel any forgiveness or kinship with Germans of my generation who, although only of school age at the time Hitler came to power, continued to follow their Führer blindly and went on to perpetrate unspeakable crimes against my people and against humanity as a whole. There is no forgiveness for them or for their parents.

Our group meets every two to three weeks. The dialogue sometimes becomes heated. The young Germans often resent the guilt they themselves feel. They make the point, clearly, that the Holocaust must never be forgotten, but that their generation is not to blame, although they almost want to share some of the responsibility.

Many have tried to make amends by doing volunteer work in Israel and other countries as part of a kind of "Peace Corps." Several people at the German Consulate work tirelessly to help survivors with problems, to overcome the mountain of paperwork associated with reparations payments and claims. They bend over backward to cut the red tape. The German Consul hosts a reception for members of the IMAS (Immigrants Mutual Aid Society) in honor of the fiftieth anniversary of the founding of that organization. They are trying to understand, asking us to forgive, and they are still searching for answers to why their country committed these colossal crimes.

I firmly believe that this dialogue is a very useful endeavor, especially for the Jewish group who had never met the decent, cultured Germans I knew. At this juncture, it is important that they get to know them and overcome the hatred they still feel. It will be most gratifying for me to see that result evolve from our meetings. I do not believe that it serves any purpose to keep blaming those who are blameless.

We must never forget, I agree. But we must also continue to teach future generations what occurred during the Holocaust. In this way, they can guard against a repetition of that nightmare.

We must keep talking to those who want to learn and understand, and extend our hand in friendship. That is what our group has been doing and will, I hope, continue to do.

Kaliski Reunion — November 7, 1992

Sixty years ago a young woman, twenty-three years old, bright, educated, and gutsy, arrived in Berlin from Breslau (now Wroclaw). Severely handicapped by polio since the age of fifteen, she realized it might be difficult to get a teaching job. She made a decision: She would open a school of her own. With the help of friends, who supported her venture in every way, her dream came true in 1932.

Lotte Kaliski started with a small number of pupils in a suburb of Berlin. She envisioned a day school, with some classes conducted in the open air, weather permitting.

After the Nazis came to power in 1933, it became increasingly difficult for Jewish children to attend public schools. The Private Waldschule Kaliski (PRI-WA-KI) was turned into a Jewish day school, although this had not been Lotte's original intention.

The faculty was most unusual. More and more teachers were being dismissed from public schools and universities and eventually found their way to the Kaliski School. As a result, the reputation of this institution grew phenomenally.

On November 7, 1992, in New York City, we celebrated the sixtieth anniversary of our school's founding. It was our second or third reunion, but this one was special. Ninety people attended, not all of them alumni, however; friends and spouses were present as well. People came from all over the world, dispersed by the Holocaust. They came from as far away as Argentina, and as close as New York. There was a group from Israel and one from England. All age groups were represented. We were a family again.

It was a great joy to all of us that Lotte Kaliski, now in her eighties and the only surviving principal of the five Jewish schools in Berlin, was there to celebrate with us. We were kids again, as unruly as ever. It was quite a task for the first speaker to call this highly individualistic group to order. But weren't we always encouraged to express ourselves, to be outgoing? That attitude probably helped us cope with the enormous problems we had growing up in Nazi Germany.

We were celebrating another event, as well. The president of a German university, Professor Michael Daxner, along with two colleagues, had made a study of our school—its history, its personalities, and its unusual curriculum. The result of this study is contained in a book that had just been published. It is a marvelous account of the wonder of it all. What it did for us who were growing up during this horrendous period of history! The book is titled *Island of Safety*, and the school truly was that. We did have a sense of safety, of belonging. The school was an oasis of sanity in a mad world.

This book emphasizes the quality of the education we received, always with the goal of preparing us for emigration. Thus, the spoiled children of affluent upper-middle-class parents learned to peel potatoes, prepare meals, and wait on table. The girls were taught mechanics. The boys were instructed in sewing. Everyone had to learn gardening and other skills that might possibly be useful for the fresh start we would have to make in a new country.

No one knew what awaited us or what would be required. Foreign languages were stressed and taught extensively and expertly. Strong emphasis was placed on music, art, drama. Who can ever forget the wonderful original plays we staged, written by our popular French teacher, Monsieur Jacob. The scores for musicals were composed by our music teacher, Erwin Jospe. The art critics of the local Jewish newspapers were charmed and full of praise. Even the Nazi "monitors," who were looking for possible infractions, seemed pleased.

I should not forget to mention our excellent sports program. Swimming was taught in our pool, running on our track, high jumping, javelin throwing, etc. We did well at sports meets among all the Jewish schools. Just about everything we learned proved to be of considerable value in our later years.

But I must get back to our reunion.

Many of our alumni have been extremely successful, among whom are John Weitz, clothing designer and author whom I used to know well when I was about fifteen (his mother was a family friend), Mike Nichols (not present) of Elaine-May-and-Mike-Nichols fame, Michael Blumenthal, Secretary of the Treasury under Jimmy Carter, Ralph Koltai, theatrical producer and director in London, and Günther Stent, professor of biology at Berkeley. This evening, Professor Stent spoke of the time that our co-director, Dr. Henry Selver, told his father to take Günther out of the school because there was "simply no hope for him." And then there was I, who had the distinction of also being asked by Dr. Selver to leave, not because of poor grades (although they were nothing to brag about), but because of unruly behavior.

After trying another school for a few weeks, I was homesick for the familiar environment. I begged to be readmitted and promised to behave. The school relented, and I obviously must have shaped up because I did graduate with my class.

My class was one of the oldest. Only one of my classmates, Robert Sommer, showed up, and I was truly amazed how much he remembered of those past years. I learned that I always let him copy my homework, admonishing him that "it was not a good idea" because "he wouldn't learn anything copying someone else's paper." It's beyond me why anyone wanted to copy *my* homework, and it makes me think that perhaps I was not such a bad student after all.

But this was a day to reminisce, and reminisce we did. We talked about other classmates and teachers and wondered what had happened to them. How many had perished, how many had survived? We felt nothing but pride and gratitude for all our teachers who had taught us so well, and affection for all who shared our young years, our past. We recognized or failed to recognize former schoolmates. No matter, we knew we had a common bond, the Private Waldschule Kaliski, the PRI-WA-KI. We recalled events we thought had been long forgotten. And we remembered with sadness the many teachers and classmates who had not survived.

I thought especially of my heartthrob, Günther Hofstein. I had heard that he had survived the war in France. We even had an address where organizers of the reunions had sent him invitations to join us but had never received a reply. I remembered my handsome boyfriend of so very long ago—more than fifty years. We used to meet at the subway station every morning to go to school. I thought of all the opera and concert performances we had attended, all the plays and movies we saw. One night we listened to a beautiful broadcast of *Rigoletto* performed by the Berlin State Opera. I have never forgotten any of it.

I wondered whatever had happened to him and if it I would ever see him again. He left Berlin for England in April 1937, and we kept corresponding, even telephoning, which was not a small feat in those days. He sent me several recorded greetings. The last time we saw each other was in April 1938 when Günther returned to Berlin once more and then left Germany for good. Shortly thereafter I emigrated to the United States, and our lives went in different directions entirely. Like so many others, we were separated by the horror of those terrible years.

The celebration continued. It was a thrill to honor Lotte Kaliski and to feel so much affection toward so many who were present. It was a thrill to see the event written up in *The New York Times* with a picture of Lotte, Lily, and me, although not one word was repeated of anything I said during the long interview I had with the *Times* reporter. It was a thrill to watch the video of the event. And finally, it will be a thrill if one of the four film makers, who have contacted us, will produce a documentary of our school and of this reunion.

We were told by Michael Daxner that next April, in Berlin, when the translation of his book into English will be completed, an exhibition will be held, honoring the school and its founder.

Some of us are planning to attend the opening. Lotte may not join us. She has vowed never to set foot in Germany again, and so far she has not broken that promise. Will she relent?

Regardless, she will be honored in Germany, although I'm not sure

Irene, Berlin 1938   *Ernst Günther (Guy) at Kaliski School, 1936*

how she feels about that honor. We can only admire her for her outstanding achievements. And she is not finished yet. After having directed a school for children with learning disabilities in Riverdale, New York, for a number of years, as well as a Montessori School in Manhattan, she is now embarking on a new venture—a Foundation for Gifted Children, which we hope will be a success.

Although Lotte reminisced with us, she told us that she never lives in the past, only in the present and the future. A lesson to be learned by us all.

November 7, 1992, was a day to honor an unusual woman who let nothing stop her from fulfilling her dream. We salute her and thank her for helping to give us the best start in life anyone could ask for.

The evening finally came to an end, and we decided to meet again in two years for a weekend so that we can be together a little longer. I thought of all the people who attend reunions and come away disappointed and bored, vowing never to go to another one. We can't wait to see each other again.

Invitation by the City Senate of Berlin
April 1993

This April I, along with many other alumni of my Alma Mater, was invited by the City Senate to spend a week in Berlin. This invitation was in conjunction with an exhibit and publication of the book about our school, discussed at our 1992 reunion.

The title of the book, *Insel der Geborgenheit (Island of Safety)*, was finally agreed upon. The author had originally entitled it *The Golden Ghetto*, a suggestion vehemently vetoed by Lotte Kaliski, the school's founder. Under no circumstances would she allow the word "ghetto" to be associated with her school. The exhibit was scheduled to open on April 21.

The invitation included my two daughters, Bunny and Myra, and I gently put the question to them. Would they accompany me to Berlin? To my surprise and delight, they accepted the invitation with a stern "but" from Bunny: "We will come with you, Mother, but you will have to realize that we cannot run all day, the way you do."

I knew that I had to tread carefully, gingerly. And I did, very carefully. Shortly after our acceptance was received in Berlin, I was sent a request from the planners of the exhibit for pictures, documents, and memorabilia. I submitted all pertinent material and was informed that it would be put on display as the record of a typical family of a student attending the school in the thirties.

I had never imagined that there would be three large panels, tastefully arranged by the committee, narrating our family's entire history. It began with photos of my maternal and paternal grandparents, my parents with me as a baby, my birth certificate, and my old German passport with the red "J" stamped on it and the middle name "Sara," added by order of the Nazi regime for every Jewish female (males had to be named "Israel").

My personal history through all my years of growing up was there for all to see, including, unfortunately and most prominently, my final report card. At this late date, it was a source more of amusement than embarrassment. There were pictures and papers pertaining to our emigration, my wedding, a recent photo of our entire family, and finally a picture of my grandfather's grave in Berlin's Jewish cemetery, which I had visited on my last trip and this time as well.

Kaliski School reunion, April, 1993

The remainder of the exhibit contained pictures and stories from the founding of the school right up to the time it was forced to close. It is a testimony to the victory of a valiant young woman who struggled against tremendous odds, as well as documentary evidence of the end of German Jewry. Pictures of teachers and students filled us with sadness as we remembered those who did not survive.

The fate of German Jewry was decided in a mere eighty minutes at the Wannsee House, which is now a Holocaust Museum. Its co-director, a German historian and a good friend of mine, had arranged a visit to the house where I was born. As we drove up to the front door, I recognized the wrought-iron gate, though it has been more than sixty years since I lived there and saw it last. In my mind's eye, I visualized the white cloth bag hanging on the gate, filled with fresh rolls, and the bottles of milk delivered every day along with the morning paper.

The present owners, a lovely couple and their thirteen-year-old daughter, welcomed us warmly. They were intrigued to be meeting someone who had lived in their house so very long ago. They told us that American soldiers had been billeted there during the war. They had purchased the house in 1976. We were given the grand tour and were impressed with the way it had been renovated and furnished.

I had lived there as a very small child and remembered very little. The room of the sixteen-year-old son of the family looked like that of any teenager. The mess seems to be universal. We were struck by the many anti-Nazi posters and slogans covering the walls. They showed clearly where this family stood and gave some indication of the values they had instilled in their children. I regretted not meeting the young man and being able to talk with him.

When our hostess, smiling broadly, pointed out that, for her, one of the selling points of the house had been the enormous master bathroom with its large sunken tub and the black and white marble sink on chrome legs, I had a flash of recognition. Why this particular area of the house had stuck in my mind I cannot say, but it was such an unusual, oversized room that somehow it must have made an indelible impression on a tiny girl.

We then went into the garden. Lightning struck! This I remembered! Whether I had seen baby pictures of myself being balanced on my father's knee in a hammock strung between two trees, being pushed on a swing by my nanny, or sitting near one of the old trees still standing, or whether I really remembered, I cannot say.

It was a thrill for me to show my daughters where and how we lived, wondering if some of the stories they had been hearing since childhood were coming to life.

Later, when I asked for their impressions, my two daughters again displayed the differences between them in outlook and expression. Myra's opinion of my childhood home was, "What a lovely place to grow up in." Bunny, obviously unimpressed by the fairly large house and always the comedienne, quipped, "I must tell you, Mother, I expected to see a mansion!" To my astonished "Whatever gave you that idea?" she replied, "Well, you always told us you had a chauffeur and a maid!"

"And that indicated to you that we lived in a mansion?" was my incredulous reply. "Don't you realize that having domestic help was very common in homes of middle-class families in those days?"

My daughter's wonderful imagination, which had always delighted us, was at play again, as it had been so many years ago when her school assignment required telling about her parents. "My father lived on a farm," she said. No one could figure out where that notion originated.

Walking around the garden, I recalled what I had considered a funny story which I had heard many times. In view of the events of a future never dreamed of in the 1920s, it was not funny at all in its implications.

To my knowledge, very few Jews had ever lived in this area, and they were not exactly welcomed by the neighbors. That may have added to my mother's intense discomfort and dislike of the house in the suburbs, so far from the city. She was at home much of the time while my father was working downtown, and she had to deal with the insidious anti-Semitism. My father's friends and business acquaintances were predominantly gentile, and he obviously did not share her feelings. Those friendships undoubtedly helped him later to evaluate the Nazi phenomenon clearly and, being forewarned, to leave Germany at the very beginning of Hitler's rise to power.

This is the story I had been told: It seems some chickens were kept in the back garden, where vegetables were also growing. One day, the rooster wandered onto our neighbor's property, and my mother got an indignant phone call to get "that Jewish bird" out of there. I have often wondered whether this was a true story or an invented reason for her dislike of the house.

We had a very pleasant visit with those charming people. Meeting another nice German family reinforced my hope that the younger generation is indeed overcoming their horrible history.

I often recall something Myra said during our stay in Berlin, namely that she felt sorry for the two generations of Germans born after the war because they seem to apologize constantly for their nation's past.

For me it was wonderful to show my daughters all the places that held so many memories for me, the house where I was born, the playgrounds where I had played, the theaters, opera houses I had visited and the city that they had heard so much about, although much had been destroyed, of course. It was something I had wanted to do for a long time and I hope that it was a meaningful experience for them . . . .

Jennifer Is Getting Married . . . Reflections 1993

Jennifer, my eldest granddaughter, is engaged to be married, and Bunny, my eldest daughter, recently turned fifty. My first reaction is: Can this be? How can my daughter be as old as I? And how can I possibly have a granddaughter ready to be married? I'm not old enough.

After I recover from the initial shock, of course, I am happy for my

My beautiful granddaughters, Jennifer and Debbie

dear grandchild and hope with all my heart that she has made the right choice and will be happy.

This family event brings with it much reflection and reminiscing. This is surely a sign of old age! I recall my own engagement and wedding, and the sadness that overshadowed it because my grandmother could not be with us. Her letters during those terrible years (reprinted above) expressed her pain at being so far away.

None of us had ever imagined we would celebrate my engagement and marriage without her. She was the most beloved and important member of our family. How warmly she wished us well, trying not to burden us with her own fears and anguish. How longingly she asked us to write her all the details and send lots of pictures. Later, she wistfully mentioned some of the beautiful dishes, candlesticks, and other objects—some of them hers—which she recognized on the festive table setting in our photos. Through it all, somehow, in spite of all the ominous signs, we never gave up hope that someday we would see her again.

I therefore am doubly privileged. I have watched my granddaughters grow from adorable children into beautiful young women. I cannot help but think: Where has the time gone? The years flew by so quickly. Wasn't it only yesterday that my daughters were babies, that they started school, grew up, graduated high school and college, survived broken hearts, and got married?

I remember so many events during my grandchildren's growing-up years. The times they spent with me as little girls, the fun things we did together and trips we took. I remember all of the celebrations—the Bat Mitzvahs, birthdays, graduations—and how proud of them I have always been.

I now look forward to the festivities celebrating Jennifer and Paul's engagement and marriage. She grew up in a home filled with love, warmth, and understanding, and I sincerely hope that her marriage will be as happy as that of her parents. The example they have set is the best gift they could have given her. Jennifer was named after my grandmother, Jenny. May she turn out to be a little bit like her namesake. That is my dearest wish for her.

I am delighted to welcome a new male member to our very small and predominantly female family. Paul will undoubtedly provide the sometimes needed reinforcement for my son-in-law, Michael, who is usually outnumbered by all the women around him. And I hope to gain a grandson. It's a happy time for us all.

Jennifer's Wedding — March 1994

As I winged my way to California to attend Jennifer and Paul's wedding, many thoughts went through my mind. I remembered my own wedding, so simple, so small, with just a few people in attendance. We were new immigrants and didn't have much money. And my grandmother was still back in Berlin, in mortal danger. I thought of the sad letters she wrote, which I had recently translated. None of us had ever imagined that she would not be with us when I got married. She, who was so important to us all and so much loved.

Now, I was lucky enough to be able to be present at my granddaughter's wedding. I was grateful and happy and a little sad remembering all our family members who had died so tragically.

I landed at the Los Angeles airport and was met by my son-in-law. I had always enjoyed the hour-long ride along the Pacific Ocean. We finally arrived at the house. It was good to see my daughter and Jennifer and Paul and, of course, Debbie, my beautiful youngest granddaughter. Paul's family and ours spent a relaxing evening enjoying one another's company. We were an interesting and diverse mixture—Jews and Catholics, Europeans, naturalized Americans, and "natives." Everyone got along, everyone belonged here.

We met again the next day for the rehearsal dinner, given by Jennifer's aunts. Saturday was a free day for manicures, hair appointments, and whatever else one does the day before a wedding. And it poured—in Southern California! "What are we going to do if it doesn't stop?" was on everyone's mind. This was to be an outdoor wedding.

We needn't have worried. Sunday, March 20, dawned sunny and bright under a cloudless California sky. Yesterday's rain had given way to perfect weather. We made our way to the Mandalay Resort Hotel in Oxnard, situated right on the ocean front, a fairy tale setting. Everyone was here. Paul's family and friends came from England, Washington, Hong Kong. Our family arrived from Boston, Phoenix, Ohio. We were all anticipating a beautiful day and were not disappointed.

When the bridal party assembled for pictures in the magnificent hotel lobby with its curved staircase, the chandeliers suddenly began to swing. We were having a strong aftershock to the recent big earthquake.

Californians have lived with this for a long time, and their nerves are frayed. I, however, felt nothing! I thought, "Well, Jennifer's wedding is an earth-shaking event"! Pictures were being taken, and I looked with love and pride at our beautiful family, especially Jennifer and her maid of honor, her sister Debbie. The bridesmaids, most of them typical Southern California beauties, looked lovely in their dark green velvet off-the-shoulder gowns.

The photo session ended, and the next stop was the bride's suite, where all the ladies, young and old, had their hair combed properly, their makeup freshened, and where snacks were available. Soon it was time for the wedding party to be seated. Parents and grandmothers were escorted down the aisle, followed by the maid of honor, the best man, the ushers, the bridesmaids, and finally the beautiful bride, on the arm of her father, the bridegroom waiting to have her "turned over" to him. It

Jennifer and Paul after the wedding ceremony, flanked by Bunny and Michael

was a touching moment. I silently saluted her parents for having done such a marvelous job in raising this lovely young woman, not an easy task in a world of turmoil.

The setting was simply gorgeous. A chamber ensemble was playing. Jennifer was radiant and a little teary-eyed as she and Paul walked toward the clergy, a priest and a cantor, awaiting them under the chuppah, with the Pacific Ocean in the background. They were to perform the ceremony together—to pronounce these two young people from such different backgrounds "husband and wife."

As the very moving ceremony progressed, my wish for them was that their different backgrounds and religions would blend in harmony, that they could work it all out to their satisfaction with love and mutual respect for each other's beliefs and customs, and that, above all, they would be happy. They have had the best examples, growing up in loving, intact families.

The reception and dinner that followed were perfect. Speeches were made—some sentimental, some humorous. And we all danced—the Irish jig and the Israeli hora. Everyone agreed, "This was truly an ecumenical celebration."

Coming Full Circle

I have come full circle. The friend of my youth, Guy (Günther Hofstein), has come back into my life. He got in touch with me after I met his sister, Evi, at the last school reunion. Fifty-plus years have fallen away. It seems only yesterday that we parted in Berlin. We remember the plays and movies we saw, the operas we listened to, and the mornings we met in the subway station on the way to school. He remembers the time he tried to kiss me, only to get a slap in the face, an incident I have conveniently forgotten. I suppose at sixteen I wasn't ready for that kind of "intimacy!" After all, this was 1936, not 1994. How young and innocent we were.

It all ended with his leaving Germany for England and later for France, where he survived the Holocaust, living with French relatives. He eventually acquired false papers and enlisted in the French army. Letters and phonograph records with loving messages kept coming until

I left for the United States, where we were so much safer than our loved ones caught in Europe. Soon after I arrived here, the war had started, and France was occupied. All communications ended.

For his own reasons, Guy never married. This prompted the immediate comment from my daughter: "Mother, that's a red flag!" I chose to ignore her well-meant advice.

After he found me again, he lost no time in writing and calling. We talked almost daily, catching up on the lost years. I asked him to visit me in Boston. When he told me the next day that he had already booked a flight and planned to stay four weeks, I was stunned, asking myself, "Can we recapture feelings from so long ago, feelings that, after all, were experienced by mere adolescents?" We were so young and had been together for such a brief time. Our life experiences had been so different. What if we couldn't stand each other?" He told me later that he had harbored similar thoughts. Any thinking person would have.

I guess miracles can still happen. We needn't have worried. The minute he walked into the terminal at Logan Airport, and we embraced, all doubts were dispelled. And this time when he kissed me, I didn't slap his face. It was as if half a century had fallen away. And it continued that way from then on.

We picked up where we had left off. We went to the movies, saw plays, enjoyed the sights in and around Boston, delighting in each other's company. We listened to classical music, as we had done long ago. Guy brought along a tape he had recorded on his keyboard with some of the hit songs we remembered from the thirties. We listened and sang along. We were young again.

He enjoyed Boston and appreciated what it had to offer. It was a joy to show him around and introduce him to my friends. Deep down I hoped that he liked everything well enough to eventually spend the rest of his life here with me. Nothing can replace a common background, shared experiences and memories. We would see what the future would hold.

We had so much to tell each other about the events in our lives for the past fifty-five years. I, of course, being an easy talker, had no problem telling him about all my experiences. It was not quite as easy for Guy, but slowly, and sometimes painfully, I believe, he told me about all the things that had happened to him.

"As you know, I left Berlin for England to study photography, and we were still able to correspond for a short time. During vacation time in

July 1938, I met my parents in the Netherlands, planning to return to England via France.

"On August 28, 1938, I arrived in Thionville, France, for the first time, to spend a fortnight with my relatives. At the end of those two weeks, I went to the British Consulate in Paris to apply for a reentry visa, but my request was denied because my passport did not show the red 'J' (for Jew) stamped in it. Neither did it show the middle name 'Israel' that Jewish men had been forced to adopt. They took me for a 'bloody' German!

"My passport had no 'J' because it had been issued prior to the time this had been required. So a fortnight in Thionville became fifty-six years—a lifetime.

"In 1939, at the beginning of the war, I was interned in two internment camps as a German, where I remained until 1940. There were Jews as well as non-Jews in the camp, where we did very little work.

"In January 1940 I was released, thanks to the efforts of my cousin Jules, who was a physician and lieutenant in the French army. Jules prepared a counterfeit health form stating that I was ill. This made it possible for me to be released as a stateless person possessing a Nansen passport attesting to that fact.

"I stayed with my cousin at their home, just fifty kilometers southeast of Paris until the German invasion in June. We then took a suitcase and bicycle and headed south. At that time I didn't speak a word of French, so I pretended to be a deaf mute. There was no other option.

"It was utter chaos. The Stukas flew in low and attacked refugees all along the road. Between walking and hitchhiking we eventually covered the 500 kilometers to Montauban. From there we went to Montpelier, where we stayed until the invasion of southern France by the Germans in '42.

"With the help of friends, I was able to obtain a false identity card under the name of Jean-Pierre Nilles, issued by the Deuxieme Bureau (Secret Service). I then went to Toulouse, where I found work until the Liberation. With the false papers, I was one of the few German Jews working in France.

"Meanwhile, my cousin Jules had been arrested and sent to several camps, including Auschwitz/Monowitz and finally Theresienstadt. He was eventually released by the invading Russians.

"After the liberation of southern France, I volunteered for the

French army. They wanted to use me as an interpreter as I spoke German and English. I refused, always feeling that I should go back to France in case my cousin ever returned. As an interpreter, I would have had to remain in Germany past the war's end. I was stationed in Alsace from 1944 to 1945 and sent back to Toulouse, where I was discharged because of a severe case of bronchitis.

"Jules did return home. He was an awful sight to behold, weighing less than seventy-five pounds! He had fallen ill with diphtheria and was completely paralyzed. Slowly and patiently, under his guidance, I nursed him back to health. He eventually recovered and resumed work as a physician until his death in 1959.

"I owned and operated a photo store in Thionville until I retired two years ago."

I was enormously touched by Guy's story and thought how much easier my life had been here in the United States. I hope his life will be a very happy one from now on, to make up for some of the hard times he experienced in the past.

Soon, I am leaving to meet him in France, and we will drive through Italy for three weeks. I have never been there and am looking forward to sharing the experience with someone who means so much to me. For the first time, as far back as I can remember, someone else is making all the plans. There is nothing for me to do except enjoy myself. In the meantime, we have to be content with daily telephone calls.

I can hardly believe that, at our age, we have been given the chance to start a new chapter in our lives. After meeting Guy, my daughter's "red flag" warning changed to: "Mother, you deserve it!" Although I don't believe "deserving" has an bearing on one's fate, those words from a daughter were greatly appreciated.

Our First Trip — Europe 1994

This was, without a doubt, the best trip I have ever taken. Even the airline cooperated. Swissair pampers its economy-class passengers as much as American airlines do their first-class ones. After such a great flight, I took it as a personal insult that it was raining on our arrival in Luxembourg, where Guy was waiting for me. What's going on here? I thought. The heavens are supposed to be smiling today. The reception I got, however, compensated for the unfriendly weather.

We drove the short distance to Thionville. I found Guy's house utterly charming. It sits on top of a hill, on a large piece of land with flowers and fruit trees, overlooking the small town. That evening the TV news had a special meaning for us, showing all the foreign troops finally leaving Berlin fifty years after the end of the war. It was quite an event. Those years had also been so memorable for us.

The next morning we loaded the little Peugeot and set out for Switzerland. Guy was going to show me a small part of Europe that was very familiar to him. After driving through the lovely countryside of France and Germany, with unavoidable traffic jams that made me feel quite at home, our first stop was Lucerne. We found a room in a hotel overlooking the beautiful lake with the sun dancing on the water's surface and the clearly visible mountains.

The food was marvelous, too much so for my diet-conscious body and mind. But I had decided to ignore the guilt feelings.

When we started toward Italy the next morning, we drove across the 6600-foot St. Gotthard Pass, and I, the worst backseat driver, felt no anxiety having someone else drive across this winding road with hairpin curves. We continued on the *Autostrada* to Milan. I was impressed by the skillful driving I witnessed, people driving an average of ninety mph. There is much more discipline on the roads here than in the States. No passing on the right is allowed, which makes driving much more orderly. People signal when they want to pass and again when they move back into the right lane. No problem. No honking.

We drove through several semi-covered tunnels, the roofs sloping away from the highway to divert possible avalanches. The toll roads use automated systems, saving a lot of time.

We did what tourists do in Milan. I don't have to talk about the museums, the statues, the palaces, or La Scala, where orchestra seats now sell for up to $500 each. Nevertheless, performances are usually sold out. Amazing!

Milan is a beautiful, interesting city, and I enjoyed the sights. Clothes were fashionable and tastefully displayed, with prices to match those of the seats at La Scala. We stuck to window shopping, but it was a pleasure to see all the stylish clothes. The natives obviously can afford the prices; we noticed many extremely well-dressed people.

The next stop was Florence. What can one say about this city that hasn't been said before? It's an "arts paradise," with many wonderful museums, especially the Uffizzi, where people stand in line for hours to get in. The palazzos, the "Pieta," the "David," as well as fashionable stores with attractive window displays. Again, we confine ourselves to window shopping.

Seeing police vans parked in front of the magnificent old synagogue, guarding it constantly, was most upsetting to me. But we soon saw that these security measures were being taken in most other European cities as well.

Our next stop, Venice, did not disappoint. Isn't this the honeymooners' paradise? So much to see, to admire. We did all the touristy things. We walked to the Ponte Rialto, rode the *vaporetti* (water taxis) packed with wall-to-wall people most of the time, the only practical way to get around in Venice. We rode up and down the Canale Grande, admiring all the old houses lining it.

On the Piazza San Marco, with its inevitable pigeon population, we acted like dumb tourists and ordered iced tea at the outdoor café to the tune of 11,000 lira (approximately $8). We should have known better.

I have never seen anything more magnificent than the mosaics of gold and glass inside San Marco basilica.

On our way back to France, we drove through part of the Dolomites, across the Brenner Pass to Innsbruck, got a $50 fine for passing where we weren't supposed to, handed to us by an obnoxiously polite Austrian policeman, who was delighted to collect this outrageous sum from a foreigner.

Continuing across the Austrian Alps and through the Arlberg tunnel, we drove through Switzerland, walked along the Bodensee in Kreuzlingen close to the German border.

Guy wanted to show me where he had been at boarding school. *Glarisegg* was situated on a magnificent estate. The director was happy to welcome an alumnus, possibly a willing contributor to the school. Guy did not oblige!

We drove on to the Rheinfall (miniature Niagara Falls) at Schaffhausen. After spending the night close by, we finally arrived back in Thionville, exhausted but happy.

In the next few days I met some of Guy's family and friends from the Flying Club, where he usually spends his afternoons. For a special treat, he took me up twice in a little four-seater plane. The weather was glorious. I was exhilarated and felt free as a bird, soaring high above the land.

Soon it was time for me to return home, reluctantly, but knowing that in a few weeks we would be together again in Boston.

I can't remember any trip I enjoyed more. It will always be a lovely memory.

Irene and Guy's wedding, December 1, 1994, with Michael, Bunny and Myra

The Wedding Announcement — December 1994

Written by Myra

*Family and friends
Were stunned and enthralled
By the news they heard
When Irene and Guy called.
After fifty-five years
Of being apart,
Guy found Irene
And stole her heart.
They're happy to announce
They tied the knot
And together found the joy
That each had sought.*

Irene Woods and Guy Hofstein

*Married on December 1, 1994,
and will make their home in
Brookline, Massachusetts*

No — The Honeymoon Is Not Over!

April 1995

Guy and I began our honeymoon in September 1994 in France, Switzerland, and Italy. We continued it in November in Boston and decided to get married on December 1. Now, of course, we had to have another honeymoon. Everybody has to have one after the wedding, *n'est-ce pas*?

We first traveled to New York and Washington and a few weeks later to San Francisco, then to Los Angeles to visit Bunny and Michael, and to San Diego for a visit with my granddaughter, Debbie. Everything was too perfect.

Finally, we settled down in Boston to some semblance of everyday life. I had stopped keeping a strict diet in Europe during the summer and continued on that regime. Lo and behold, my cholesterol level hadn't gone up, and neither had my weight. It was too difficult to watch my husband eating all the "forbidden" food without any concern and looking at me with a quizzical, somewhat pitying look when I worried about weight and cholesterol. He wisely decided to say nothing. No one in Europe seems to share the American preoccupation with all sorts of diets. I have often wondered about the statistics and whether Europeans have a higher incidence of deaths due to heart attacks than we have here in the United States.

At the end of March, after finally getting a permanent resident card, Guy returned to France to take care of some business, and I followed at the beginning of April. We worked hard to dismantle his house in Thionville, packing and preparing for shipment everything that was to go to Boston.

Our honeymoon continued. We had planned to go to a health spa on the coast of Britanny that Guy had enjoyed for the past twenty-five years with excellent results. It was a first for me, but he promised me a miracle cure for everything that ailed me, and I was willing to be shown.

After an eight-hour drive, we arrived in Quiberon. I was impressed by the beautiful hotel. Our room had a balcony with a magnificent view of the Atlantic. A large bowl of fruit and a bouquet of flowers greeted us. I was surprised by this touch of personal attention, but was told that all the steady patrons are treated this way.

The food was outstanding and, as is customary in Europe, the portions mercifully small. It was a pleasure to sit in the attractive dining room overlooking the water and watch the sun set over the ocean.

The health treatments were scheduled to begin in the morning after an examination by a physician, who prescribed which "torture" one had to submit to. I was not as happy with the entire procedure as Guy had obviously been, returning for so many years. But it was a luxurious, if sometimes very exhausting, two weeks. I was no worse, and no better for the experience. The only activity I enjoyed was swimming in the Olympic-size pool and—ah!—the massages. We lucked out and were assigned the best masseur in the whole place. I loved the walks we took along the shore, even though there were many reminders of the war, such as old bunkers of the German Atlantic Wall. I inspected everything with great interest.

We returned to Thionville to pick up the luggage we had left in Guy's house. Finally, we arrived in Boston. My back still hurt, as did my shoulder. I guess I'll have to stick to the old remedies of anti-inflammatories and whatever else has helped me in the past. Acupuncture has done wonders for me.

Regardless, it was a lovely trip, and I will remember it fondly, even without the promised "miracle cure."

Chicago — November 4, 1995

We are having a great, fun-filled weekend in Chicago. What an exciting, beautiful city. We have taken a tour, run around all day, and finally made it back to our hotel. We are tired and frozen from the bone-chilling cold. We put up our feet, flip on the news, and time stands still, as it did so long ago on another November day more than thirty years ago.

"Prime Minister Yitzhak Rabin of Israel has been assassinated" is the first news we hear. And what goes through our minds immediately? "Those damn Arabs! Now there will be another war in the Middle East." The news continues: "The Prime Minister was gunned down by a Jewish law student as he left a peace rally—by a religious fanatic opposed to the peace process."

We are stunned. Thoughts are jumbled in my head. "Luckily it was not an Arab; at least for now there will not be another war. But how can a Jew kill another Jew, the leader of his country? This just doesn't happen!" Slowly, we try to sort out the enormity of this crime. New pain has been inflicted on world Jewry.

This affects not only Israelis but Jews all over the world, many of whom will always regard Israel as their country, too. Whether we are Americans, Frenchmen, or Britons, the land is dear to our hearts. We have seen it develop over these past fifty years from a desert to a beautiful, vibrant, productive country, and in one way or another, we have helped.

My first emotion is rage. Rage against the religious right. The assassin's declaration, "God told me to do it" and his fellow fanatics' glee that Rabin was dead, again confirms my conviction that zealots of any religion will in the end bring down world order in the name of God, Allah, or whomever they pray to. And there was rage against the Israeli security forces, supposedly the best in the world. How could they have let this happen?

Strangely enough, my second emotion was pain and regret that I was not at home. I thought I would probably have gone to some memorial service to be with fellow Jews. My feeling of belonging to the Jewish people has always emerged strongly on such occasions.

I had to talk to someone who, I knew, would share my feelings. I called my elder daughter, Bunny, and we cried together, as we had done when Kennedy was killed, and she was the first one to call me at my office, in tears. We talked about that terrible day, about the days afterward when no one moved away from the TV, when the nation stood still, and together we mourned. We imagined it would be the same in Israel.

The official mourning period would be seven days, the week of Shiva that Jews observe. We knew we would be up at dawn to watch the funeral ceremonies in Jerusalem.

Again, as so many years ago, I could not tear myself away from the television set. The spectacle of seeing so many world leaders, former enemies, paying tribute to an Israeli Prime Minister filled me with pride. We watched Leah Rabin, the Prime Minister's widow, shaking her head in disbelief and reluctantly shaking hands with Benjamin Netanyahu, whom she would later accuse of bearing some responsibility for the tragedy that befell her, her family, and her country. He, as the political leader of the religious right, had done nothing to stop the inflammatory talk of his followers. How could an Israeli stand by while the Prime Minister of his country is pictured in a Nazi uniform?

We missed not one minute of the funeral services. We watched the Rabin family comfort one another as best they could. There was none of the pageantry that was so outstanding at Kennedy's funeral, but the service was impressive, simple, and dignified.

The eulogies by the various dignitaries showed the esteem held for Rabin by everyone. He had appeared to be so serious and sober a figure, that I had never imagined such an outpouring of sentiment and grief. There was much we did not know about this man—publicly and privately. Every speaker revealed a different facet of his personality.

Clinton's remarks were warm and moving. The humorous anecdote about the Prime Minister being unable to tie his tie because he was not used to wearing one, brought smiles to all who grieved. Clinton's farewell in Hebrew, "Shalom, Chaver," pronounced correctly, was touching. We saw a president who was not afraid to show his feelings for a friend.

To hear King Hussein of Jordan speak of his former enemy as "my friend" was most reassuring. The peace process with Jordan will hold! The king recalled the assassination of his grandfather, which he had witnessed as a small boy so many years ago. He also had tried to achieve peace in the Middle East.

But nothing could surpass the wonderful tribute by Yitzhak Rabin's eighteen-year-old granddaughter. Her farewell revealed to the world the private person, the husband, father, grandfather, and what he meant to his family. All of us wept with this beautiful young girl, trying to cope with her first great loss.

Finally, the casket was borne to the Mount of Olives where so many great Israelis are buried. Ted Kennedy, with his son at his side, had brought soil from his brother's grave at Arlington National Cemetery and mixed it with soil that was to cover the grave of another World Leader, gunned down in a mindless crime. He could surely feel the pain of the Rabin family and the Israeli people.

Will this latest violence have been in vain? Or will it finally lead to peace? Will the "silent majority," who always need to be shaken up, finally be silent no longer? Will the zealots be told by their "God" to live by human laws and stand up to those who kill in his name? How long will it go on. . . in the name of God?

Losses — February 1996

As we grow older, our circle of friends and family grows ever smaller. During the past year three people who have been an important part of my life have died.

My maternal aunt, aged ninety-four, who was very close to me during my childhood until she left Germany for Palestine as soon as Hitler came into power, when I was twelve years old. She had taken me in when my mother and I couldn't cope with each other, which was not infrequently. It was thanks to her that we were able to get out of Germany in time to come to this country. She had moved to the United States with my uncle and cousin in 1937. In spite of the fact that she became quite difficult in her later years, I have never forgotten how much I owe her. The fond feelings remained.

My dear friend, Lotte Kaliski, also died recently. She had understood the problems of my adolescent years and was always ready and willing to listen and help. It is only recently that I found out from the book that was written about her and her school that her life had been somewhat similar to mine. She also was a child of divorce and had difficulty getting along with her mother. It explained a lot. Her understanding came from similar experiences.

After she came to the United States and settled in New York, she opened a school for children with learning disabilities and called it the New Kaliski School. It was located on a large estate in Riverdale and resembled the old one in many ways. When she began to have difficulties obtaining funding from the State of New York, she asked me if I would like to do something for my "old teacher."

She wanted me to do recruiting for the school, contacting child psychiatrists and psychologists who could refer to her young patients in need of special education. I was, of course, glad to oblige, and I believe that I was successful in getting quite a few students to enroll.

Lotte and I had become good friends by that time. The age difference, which had seemed enormous when I was fourteen and she was twenty-six, was nothing now, and I was eager to repay her for all she had done for me.

She died this year after many years of illness and suffering, which she had borne with feistiness and a lot of anger. Another important person connected with my past, someone I will always remember not only with affection, but also with admiration for her achievements in the face of enormous odds.

The most recent death that touched me deeply was that of my employer for over twenty-five years, who had also been a good friend and adviser, especially after my first husband died many years ago.

When I entered the beautiful church for his memorial service a few weeks after he was buried, I felt very sad, although I had not seen him for many years. The minister spoke of him with great warmth and humor, relating little anecdotes, describing the dedicated physician, the family man, and the many activities in which he was involved.

I was moved to tears, however, by the eulogy given by his eldest granddaughter. She lovingly painted a portrait of a caring, involved grandfather. Here was a different side of the man I had known professionally for so many years. My thoughts wandered back to the beginning. As long as I could think, I had always wished to be a doctor. There was, of course, no chance to realize that dream after the Nazis came to power. Jews could not attend universities or obtain a higher education. Today, I know that it would not have made any difference. Looking at an old report card with my grades, and knowing my lack of staying power, patience, and attention span, I would never have made it. I remained fascinated by the medical field, however, and when I was ready to go to work after my children were in school (I had worked a bit all along, dabbling in all kinds of things), I answered an ad: "Medical secretary wanted, medical terminology required." I had hardly any knowledge of medical terms, but, being gutsy, I responded to the ad and got the job. One day a week I worked with the doctor's wife, who did the bookkeeping at home in a basement office. She was a member of the DAR (Daughters of the American Revolution), a term which was new to me then. She would never even offer me, a Jewish woman, a cup of tea. But I was determined to stick it out in order to learn. Two days a week I worked in the doctor's office, transcribing medical histories, bluffing my way through, with the help of the very nice girls working there. Eventually, I became very proficient in my work.

Now I was ready to apply for another job. I was hired immediately by an older secretary who had worked for the doctor ever since he started to practice and had known his family for many years. The office was located in a small orthopedic hospital, and I learned that I was the first Jew that had ever been allowed to enter those hallowed halls. Many years later the secretary told me that, before I started, she had to warn the doctor that I was Jewish, because she knew his prejudices.

As an old WASP, he liked only White Anglo-Saxon Protestants. I was dumbfounded because from the start I had experienced only kindness from him. If my presence created any discomfort for him, it was not evident. I, on the other hand, could not remember a time when I was as conscious of my Jewishness as in those first years at the Robert Brigham Hospital (now defunct) nor had I ever experienced personal discrimination except for the time I lived under the Nazis in Berlin.

I worked only mornings in order to be home when my children returned from school. As the years passed, Dr. P. came to appreciate my work, and after the old secretary retired, I was ready to work fulltime. Naturally, we got to know each other better. He was appointed Chief of Surgery, and I was in charge of the office.

I remained the only Jew in the place until I was joined eventually by two fellow Jews: a ward secretary and a surgical resident. Years later, I found out that my boss had gone to bat for the resident even though the hospital administration had been reluctant to hire him. I must have convinced this complex man that Jews did not have horns.

My attention returned to the minister's eulogy. He was speaking admiringly of Dr. P.'s definite opinions, how one could not budge him once he had taken a stand, how he always let people know what his position was, and how things should be done. I chuckled inwardly, thinking, "Not in *my* office." There *I* was boss.

My thoughts went back to the days when I set out to change this wonderful, caring surgeon's attitude toward non-WASPS. When he once mentioned "those Eyetalians," I asked him, "What's the matter, you don't like Italians, either?" I never let up, and over the years he met and got to like many of my friends and family. He once heard a eulogy given by our rabbi for a fellow surgeon and, with great admiration, he said, "I wish we had a preacher like that in our church."

One day he tried to explain where his anti-Jewish feelings had originated. (Every bigot has a rationalization.) As a resident, he had worked on the lower East Side of New York. This was his only contact with poor immigrants in that area. I asked him whether he had any idea what it was like to leave one's country and all one holds dear to begin entirely anew in a strange land without knowing the language and without money. "Wouldn't you use your elbows to get ahead under such circumstances?" was my question. I had made my point.

When I turned sixty, I was ready to retire and, being sixty-nine, the doctor decided he might as well do the same. He wasn't going to be one of those "old doctors roaming the corridors of the hospital and have everyone asking, 'Is he still around?'"

He owned a house "up country" in New Hampshire and looked forward to fishing, skiing, and woodworking, and we began to wind up the practice. The remaining papers were packed and brought home.

For a while, I continued to do some work at his home in Newton, and on one of the last days, when everything was packed, he presented me with a beautiful brass menorah, explaining that he had bought it in a pawn shop on the East Side many years before, and wanted me to have it. I was deeply touched and gratified. I had converted one anti-Semite, even if it was only a drop in the bucket.

As we filed out of the church after the service, I met the "young"—now quite gray—surgeon Dr. P. had sponsored so long ago. He also recalled him fondly, acknowledging how much he had been helped during his first difficult years of residency. I said good-bye, feeling sad but also elated.

Israel — March 1996

I had been in Israel before. The first time was right after the 1967 war when I rode a bus on the same road where another bus had been blown up the previous day. I never gave it a second thought. This time it was different. Was it because I am older and not as daring as I once was? Was it that my life is such a happy one now that I'm afraid to lose it? Or was it that the attacks are now so much more cruel, occurring in the center of the cities? I must admit that, on the eve of our departure, I had had thoughts of possibly not coming back, of being killed. It was a strange way of embarking on a "pleasure" trip! The start of Guy's and my journey was not encouraging. The weather had been beautiful all week, but snow fell all day on the day of our departure. We boarded the plane, but then sat on the runway for an hour until we were informed that, due to snow on the wings, a full load of fuel would not last until London. It would be necessary to land in Gander (Newfoundland) to refuel. Our connection in London to Tel Aviv looked dim. Indeed we were delayed long enough to miss it. Not a good beginning!

British Airways put us up for the day in a nice hotel near the

London airport and rebooked us for a flight leaving at 10:40 P.M. Again, we boarded on time . . . and we sat . . . . Finally, an announcement was heard: A passenger who was booked on the flight and had already been checked in, had decided not to fly, which meant that her four pieces of luggage had to be found and taken off the plane. No unaccompanied luggage may be left on any flight. Needless to say, this took another ninety minutes, and I grew more apprehensive. Was this a bad omen? Was this trip necessary?

We finally landed in Tel Aviv at 6:00 A.M., about thirty-six hours after leaving Boston. We could have flown to Australia in that time. It took most of the day to collect ourselves and catch up on lost sleep.

In the middle of the afternoon, police cars and ambulances began racing by, sirens screaming. We knew that something serious had happened—again.

We soon learned that not far from the hotel, at Diezengoff Center, one of the busiest places in the city, another fanatic had blown himself up on a crosswalk with a bomb laced with nails, and that there were many casualties, mainly young people and children in costume for the Purim holiday.

Everyone was stunned. Many phone lines were down and others jammed. Some of the hotel personnel were frantic to get in touch with their families. I tried to call home to reassure my daughters, but there was no way to get through. They finally reached us and begged us to come home.

In spite of the seriousness of the situation, I had to chuckle. Only three days before, I had had a long conversation with Bunny, voicing concern. The answer I got was, "Well, Mother, then you can't go to London or Paris, either. Things are happening all over the world!" I had agreed, but now here she was telling us to come home. However, we had no intention of cutting short our visit.

As it turned out, very few tourists were leaving. There were cancellations from some Americans, but everyone else seemed to be remaining. Many groups continued their planned tours of the country.

In spite of my daughter's orders not to use public transportation, we did ride a bus the day after the attack and passed the site of the tragic bombing. I will never forget the horror we felt. Many store windows were blown out and the stores were in shambles. The scene was one of desolation, but it was amazing how much had already been cleaned up in that short time. We thought mostly of the lives that had been lost. Candles and flowers had been placed in various spots.

In the days that followed, life went on in an amazingly normal manner. Buses were not quite as crowded as usual, but not for long. We had the greatest admiration for the people and how they coped with recurring tragedies. A planned young people's concert went on as scheduled and was well attended. It had been decided not to deprive the children of their holiday pleasure. It was, after all, Purim today!

We also attended a philharmonic concert that evening and, despite our apprehension before coming to Israel, we adopted the attitude of the population. We went about our business normally, trying not to think about the danger lurking at every corner. Yet, how many times have we told ourselves, "We can go home if we choose to, but they have to stay and live with this constantly. But life goes on. How do they manage it?"

Am I Really Seventy-five Years Old?

That's the question I ask myself as I celebrate seventy-five long years. How lucky I have been. I escaped with my life two months before World War II erupted, and the destruction of Europe as we knew it, from a country we loved. A war would be started again by Germany, barely twenty years after the end of World War I. Who could possibly have imagined the horrors that were to follow?

Reflecting on my life with gratitude, I think of all the people we loved, young and old, whose lives were extinguished. I view my happiness. I have found the friend of my youth. After all these years, we have been given another chance. We have been allowed to begin a new chapter in our lives at the age of seventy-five.

Although my younger daughter has sweetly told me that I "deserved" it all, I am not quite comfortable with that statement. I think of all our loved ones who "deserved" to live, especially my grandmother, who was so good. Did she "deserve" to come to such a horrible end? And how about my beautiful girlfriend Marianne, whose exquisite singing voice could have given pleasure to so many? And all the others, too numerous to mention. All those innocent millions. Thinking of them will always throw a cloud over my happiness. None of them "deserved" their fate.

Today I also remember that hot, humid day in August when my

mother and I arrived in New York. We were overwhelmed by the heat, noise, and dirt, but we soon continued on to Boston, which was indeed a livable city. The difficulties we encountered, not knowing the language, were soon overcome by evening language classes. I never wanted to repeat the embarrassing experience when a kind young girl invited me for an evening out with a group of young people my age, and I sat there like a lump, unable to join the conversation. That this could happen to me!

The country was in a depression, and jobs were hard to find, but we managed. We had no choice, having arrived with $10 in our pocket. Soon I found a job with the impressive salary of $12 a week. But with milk, for example, costing only nine cents a quart, we managed quite well.

After a few months, I decided it might be a good idea to get married. I met a very nice young man, and my dream came true. I was nineteen years old and no more ready for marriage than the man in the moon, but luckily my fiancé, Egon, was nine years older and a bit wiser. At our wedding we felt the absence of friends and family more keenly than at any other time. We thought of them all as they were thinking of us, judging by the many letters we received, expressing their frustration at being unable to attend our wedding.

With our combined salaries, $17 a week each—a small fortune in those days—we were able to rent a very nice two-bedroom apartment. We continued to work and save money. Yes, one actually saved money in those days. In a few years, our first little daughter was born, and the second followed four years later. Two children, just as I had planned; our family was complete.

By now, my husband had a good job, and we had saved enough to move from our third-floor walkup to a lovely three-bedroom apartment in a two-family house in the Brighton section of Boston, where the children had many playmates. Those were good years. Our marriage lasted twenty-eight years until my husband's untimely death in 1968. He had never been able to overcome the trauma of being incarcerated in a concentration camp, even if it had only been for a short time.

Our two "native-born" children helped us integrate completely into the American way of life. They gave us so much joy, along with the usual aggravations, through the years of grammar school, high school, college, boyfriends, broken hearts, marriages, and also divorces. I remember it all today.

I recall the many fun things we used to do together: trips we took, the time Bunny, at age fourteen, decided to run away at Passover and packed matzoth, as if we were so religious she couldn't have eaten bread. I was frantic, but her father knew where to look for her. Perhaps I had been too nonchalant when she told me she was leaving, telling her I would help her pack, never dreaming that she was serious. How guilty I felt. We found her in the local movie theater with a suitcase filled with sweaters (in case she had to camp out) and the matzoth.

And I remember how many times we had told her not to go to school via the high cliff behind our house, finding out later that she had not only continued to take the shortcut but had taken her younger sister, who was petrified of heights. Then there was the time Dad decided to fix her up for a date. Always the comedienne, when she came home she said, "Daddy, please forget my phone number."

Myra was the quiet one of the family. Will I ever forget the postcard she wrote to us from a Jewish summer camp, which read: "They are too cheap here to give us milk with our meals, all we get is punch!" How was she to know that milk with a meat dish was not kosher? She had never experienced a kosher home. There was so much more. How can I recount it all here? The pleasures always outweighed the aggravations.

Now there are two granddaughters, one already married, and their mother is going through some of the problems her mother faced a few years back. It all goes around, does it not?

My life alone for twenty-five years was always busy, interesting, and challenging, with many friends, lots of activities and trips. I never felt lonely and was quite content, not realizing what I was missing.

Now Guy has come back into my life and made it complete. All the years have fallen away, but, unfortunately, not the wrinkles. Yes, both of us are older, much older, but in each other's eyes we still see the young sixteen-year-olds who dated, more or less carefree, during the Nazi years in Berlin. Each of us has made a life since. Mine was the happier one.

He lived under the German occupation in France, spent time in holding camps, went underground with false papers, always afraid of discovery, fleeing from the Germans part of the time. How lucky I had been in comparison, living in this country.

We are now trying to compensate for all those lost years, trying to recapture much of what was lost. We are doing all the things we used to do together so long ago. We attend concerts, see plays, go to the movies, and enjoy life to the fullest. We have revisited many of the places in Berlin, where we were happy before the world erupted.

On this day of my seventy-fifth birthday, I thank my fate for having dealt with me so kindly. My cup runneth over.

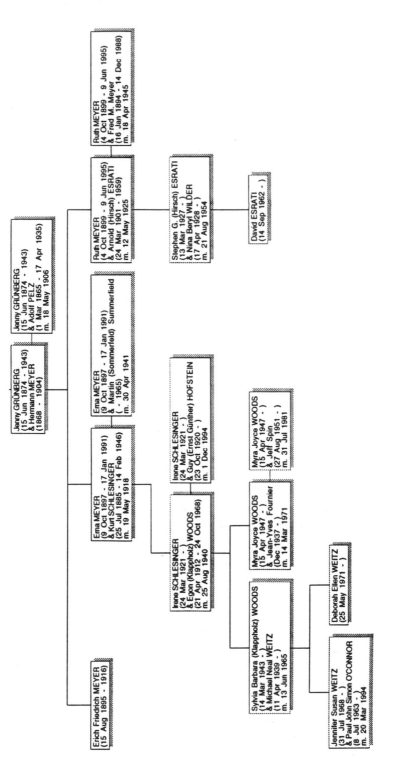

The Pelz/Schlesinger family tree

People Mentioned in the Text

Jenny Pelz, née Gruenberg, b. June 15, 1874, Schoenlanke, Germany. Murdered in Auschwitz, sometime in 1944. First marriage to Hermann Meyer, who died at age 36. They had three children: Erich, died in WWI. **Erna**, addressed in the letters as **Ernilein**, **Ruth** (**Ruthelein**). Second marriage to **Adolf Pelz**, called **Vati** in letters. He died of lung cancer in Berlin in 1935, was buried at the Jewish cemetery in Berlin-Weissensee.

Irene (**Reni, Renilein**), writer of this book. Daughter of Erna Meyer and Kurt Schlesinger, b. March 24, 1921, Berlin-Zehlendorf. Immigrated to the United States, August 1939, with her mother, Erna. M. Egon Klappholz (Woods), August 25, 1940. Two daughters, Sylvia Barbara (Bunny), b. March 14, 1943, and Myra Joyce, b. April 15, 1947, Boston, Massachusetts.

Erna Summerfield, née Meyer, b. October 9, 1897 in Berlin, Germany. M. Kurt Schlesinger, May 1918, divorced 1924. One daughter, Irene. Immigrated to the United States, August 1939, m. Martin Summerfield (Sommerfeld) in 1941 in Boston, d. January 17, 1991, in Needham, Massachusetts.

Kurt Schlesinger b. July 25, 1884, Berlin, Germany. M. Erna Meyer 1918, divorced 1924. M. Christine (Christl) Dahlhausen 1929. Immigrated to Amsterdam, Netherlands, in 1933. Incarcerated at Camp Westerbork for a short time, freed by his non-Jewish wife, d. in Amsterdam in automobile accident in 1946.

Egon Klappholz (**Woods**), b. April 21, 1912, in Königshütte (now Królewska Huta), Upper Silesia. Incarcerated in Buchenwald on Kristallnacht in 1938 and subsequently released. Immigrated to the United States in March 1939. Died October 24, 1968 in Brookline, Massachusetts.

Ruth (**Ruthelein**) **Meyer**, b. October 4, 1899, Berlin, Germany. m. Arnold Hirsch May 12, 1925, Berlin. Immigrated to Palestine in 1933 w.

Arnold and son, Stefan. Name changed to **Esrati**. Came to the U.S. in 1937. Subsequently divorced Arnold. m. Fred M. Meyer, April 18, 1946, Boston. d. 1995, Cleveland, Ohio.

Arnold (Arne) Hirsch, b. March 24, 1901, Dortmund, Germany. m. Ruth Meyer May 12, 1925 Berlin., immigrated to Palestine 1933, name changed to **Esrati**. Came to the U.S. in 1937 and brought Erna and Irene over. Subsequently divorced Ruth. Died in Israel 1959.

Stefan Hirsch (Step, Steppke) (now Stephen), son of **Ruth** and **Arnold (Arne) Hirsch.**, b. March 13 1927 Berlin. Immigrated to Palestine in 1933 changed name to **Gideon Esrati**. Came to the U.S. in 1937.

Claere or **Clara (Hirsch)**, Arnold's mother, died in Theresienstadt.

Hanna (Schlesinger) and Max Pelz. Kurt's sister, married to Adolf's brother. Daughter **Susanne (Susi)**. They all died in Auschwitz.

Arthur and **Jeanette Pelz**. Adolf's brother and his wife. Both killed in Auschwitz.

Fritz Schlesinger, brother of Kurt, perished in Lódz, Poland, along with his son, **Klaus**. His wife, **Margaret**, escaped to England.

Edith and **Erich Schlesinger**, Kurt's cousins. Erich died in Theresienstadt, along with Edith's mother. Edith was sent to Auschwitz then liberated, and made her way back to Berlin. She eventually came to the United States and died in New York in her nineties.

Paula and Sigmund (Ebenstein). Old friends whose son, **Alfred**, immigrated July 10, 1940 to the United States. Despite his efforts to bring his parents here, they were deported to Theresienstadt and later to Auschwitz.

Willi (Bukofzer). Old friend in whose apartment Jenny rented a room after she was forced to give up her apartment. Because of great difficulties with Willi, she eventually moved out.

Mille and Adolf (Aufrecht). Old friends with whom Jenny lived after she moved out of Willi's apartment until she was deported to

Theresienstadt. Their son **Pepi** was a good friend of Irene's. He and his brothers all left Germany and came to the United States.

Antonia (Toni, Anton) Schulze. A former employee, later a friend of Jenny's, who helped her until Jenny's deportation, at great danger to herself. Added Jenny's name to that of her beloved husband, Adolf, on his gravestone, with the inscription "Murdered in Auschwitz in 1944."

Jenny (Frohmann). Old family friend who emigrated to Amsterdam very early in the 1930s. Was in Theresienstadt with Jenny (Pelz) and tried desperately, through an acquaintance, to keep her out of the Auschwitz transport, but without success and she left on the last transport to Auschwitz. Letters by Jenny Frohmann, who was liberated and returned to Amsterdam, tell us of her last days.

Betty, Bernhardt, Lisa, Helga (Meyer). Aunt, uncle, and cousins, also living in Amsterdam. In hiding for some time before parents were discovered. Lisa and Helga survived and are still living in Amsterdam. **Hulda (Gruenberg)** Betty's mother.

Herta and Willy Friedland. Herta was an old school friend of Erna's. **Marianne**, their daughter, 'Reni's best friend. All of them, including their son **Bobby**, were murdered in Auschwitz.

Lore (Pickardt) Gruen. Friend of Reni's, survived the war in Berlin, saved from deportation by her gentile mother. She recently died of cancer. Her husband, **Heinz Gruen**, also survived in Berlin, also a *Mischling* (one non-Jewish parent). Still lives in Berlin.

Hina (Mrs. Hinze). Our former seamstress. **Ruth,** her daughter.

Most of the other names are friends and acquaintances.

Guy Hofstein, b. October 23, 1920, as **Ernst Günther** in Leipzig, Germany. M. Irene (Schlesinger) on December 1, 1994, in Brookline, Massachusetts.